"Pastor, We Need to Talk!"

How congregations and pastors can solve their problems before it's too late

Dennis J. Hester

"Pastor, We Need to Talk!"

How congregations and pastors can solve their problems before it's too late

Published by His Way Publishing, Winston-Salem, NC
Email: customerservice.ebooks@gmail.com

Every effort has been made to be accurate in quoting and sharing the ideas and writings of those quoted in this book. An apology is in order for errors or any inaccuracies that the reader may discover. Readers are encouraged to contact the author at His Way Publishing with suggested corrections.

Second Edition Second Printing 2015
Cover design by Ted Ferguson Cover photo by Dean Davis
Interior formatting and typesetting by PenworthyLLC
Printed in USA by Createspace

Library of Congress Control Number: 2001087794

ISBN: 978-0-9709580-2-0

Disclaimer

This book is published to encourage, support, educate and motivate congregations, church leaders and staff to build stronger relationships with one another and to work to find effective alternatives to terminating church staff and hurting one another.

This book is only a guide, filled with suggested strategies and resources in managing and resolving conflict. It is not the last word in dealing with conflict.

The author and His Way Publishing shall have neither liability nor responsibility to any person or church with respect to any loss or damage caused, or alleged to have been caused, directly or indirectly, by the information contained in this book.

This book is sold with the understanding that neither the author nor the publisher is engaged in rendering legal or other professional service. If legal advice or other expert assistance is required, the services of a competent professional person should be sought.

DEDICATION

I dedicate this book to Jesus Christ my personal Saviour and the Lord of my life. I commit this book to Him who has allowed me to be a part of the family of God.

My wife, Pam, my best friend and my biggest fan who said "yes" in 1986 to our becoming a family, I love you and thank you for your support.

Nathan, my son, who encouraged me to get on with writing this book when he asked, "Dad, why are you always writing great titles, but never writing any books?"

My daughter, Rachael, who reminded me often while writing this book to take a break from working when she proclaimed, "Dad, you need some fun in your life!"

To Bud and June Hester (Mom & Dad) who gave me roots and wings and loved me and supported me in whatever I felt God was calling me to do.

And especially to these church families that I have had the pleasure to serve:

Jonesboro Baptist Church	Roseland, VA
Pioneer Baptist Church	Varania, VA
Zoar Baptist Church	Shelby, NC
Mount Pleasant Baptist Church	Mooresboro, NC
Cherokee Creek Baptist Church	Gaffney, SC
Broad River Baptist Church,	Blacksburg, SC
Camps Creek Baptist Church	Mooresboro, NC
Union Cross Baptist Church	Kernersville, NC

FOREWORD

Heavenly horse sense is rare. That's why a book that blends the mystical heart and the methodical head is so timely and so needed by our congregations.

Our churches hunger for mystics and methodicals when conflict stirs. Mystics seek God's will first, last, always. They believe the Golden Rule and biblical principles guide daily living. Methodicals search for levels, procedures, problem-solving options, research reports, and outside consultants. Both mystics and methodicals can lead their congregations toward health and toward effective future ministries—if they hear and follow their hearts and heads faithfully.

Thanks, Dennis. Your practical coaching points give us hope and map healing processes for our congregational dialogues. *"Pastor, We Need to Talk!"* sets the stage for finding and doing the will of God. May God bless our talking and listening and discerning.

Bob Dale
Center for Creative Church Leadership Development
Richmond, VA
November 2000

PREFACE

If you have purchased this book, you are probably hurting or know someone or some congregation that is hurting. Or you may sense the brewing of a potential conflict that could bring disunity, embarrassment and pain to you or your congregation. It is my desire that this book will become a tool that God will use in the life of individuals and congregations to bring about healing.

This book is a resource tool. I hope it will challenge you to think, to dialog, reflect and to discover insights about your relationships as church leaders and congregational members. It is my prayer that you will internalize these truths and principles and apply them daily in every area of your life, as well as at church. This book invites you to start a conversation with your church leaders and laity that will be ongoing. You will be encouraged to study patterns of behavior that cause you to find yourself and your congregation in conflicting situations. But more so, this book gives some "do's" and "don'ts" of preventive medicine that can keep you and your church from allowing conflict to destroy relationships and ministry. Openness, honesty, and humility can help you discover these truths and apply the instructions listed here.

"Pastor, We Need To Talk!" is obviously not an exhaustive study in conflict management and resolution. More extensive studies have been written on this topic. Suggested resources are listed in the appendix and also on the author's website, *www.Peoplepowertraining.com*.

When a person or a group is in conflict, help is needed quickly. *"Pastor, We Need To Talk!"* provides some alternatives, suggestions and even study questions that individuals or congregations may find helpful. At the end of most chapters there are some realistic examples of churches and church leaders (some of them true, though the names of ministers and churches have been changed) who have experienced conflict. Peep through the window of these churches, and you just might see your pastor and your church.

The appendix is intended to be a helpful resource center. There you will find study questions, end notes and additional resources and contact information, recommended reading, surveys, selected Biblical references, and information about how the author can be of future help.

It is my prayer that "*Pastor, We Need To Talk!*" will help enable you, your pastor, church staff and your congregation to work through and to learn from your conflicts, so that you can more effectively serve in God's Kingdom.

May God bless you and your congregation as you experience

"... how good and how pleasant it is
For brothers to dwell together in unity!"
(Psalm 133:1).

ACKNOWLEDGMENTS

This book has been a kingdom effort. In reality every acquaintance, friend and foe, has contributed in some way to this book. Every conflict, relationship and experience as a neighbor, church member, or minister has been grist for the mill in writing this book.

This book would not have been possible without the friendship and help of Dr. Paul Sorrells. Throughout his life, his calling has been to serve as an English professor and as a pastor. Paul and I became friends when he was my English professor at Gardner-Webb College in 1972. He later was my pastor and has always been an encourager to me as a minister and as a writer. He has always been a mentor. I've taken his spiritual counsel seriously because he has the gift of wisdom. I've never made a major decision without first seeking his counsel. Through the years we have passionately debated numerous issues—and remained friends. During the writing and re-writing of this book, we have cri-tiqued, discussed and wrestled with this topic of conflict in the church.

In reality, Paul's name should also be on the front of this book, but in his humble and mountaineer way he kept telling me, "No, I'm just an editor; you're the writer." Paul agreed with my idea that there was a need for a book of this nature. It started out as a short booklet to be written in a few weeks, but it grew into this book that has taken a year of research and re-writing. Paul, like a prophet, has emphatically proclaimed to me time and time again: "Keep your target audience in mind, the church, and keep it short and simple. People who are angry don't want to read too much; they want help in a hurry." So here I want to acknowledge Paul's tireless editing of my spelling and grammar. Paul once told me in college, "Don't worry about not being a good speller, they have editors for that. Just learn how to put words together." I took Paul at his word.

I thank Paul for his friendship, invaluable support and help during the writing of *"Pastor, We Need To Talk!"*

- To Bob Dale, Director for the Center for Creative Church Leadership Development in Virginia, who wrote the Foreword, a hearty thanks. He is a great resource person for ministers and congregations. I have benefited from him as a former seminary professor, conference leader, and an encourager to me as a writer. His many books on church life and leadership are always practical and applicable.

- Thanks to John Savage with L.E.A.D. Consultants. Savage and those in his organization are superb trainers. His training in listening skills, leadership, and conflict management and conflict resolution has benefited me more than any training I have received as a minister. I thank Dr. Savage for writing the Afterword to this book and challenging each of us to apply our learnings.

- Through the years I have been challenged and enlightened by the writings of Warren W. Wiersbe, author of the famous "Be Series" of the New Testament. He is now in the process of writing commentaries on the Old Testament to be included in the same series. He is either the author, co-author or compiler of 150 books — at this writing. I appreciate his reading my manuscript, making suggestions and endorsing *"Pastor, We Need To Talk!"* I have especially enjoyed his *Walking with the Giants and Talking with the Giants.*

I could not have written this book without the former conversations and training from the following friends, ministers, trainers and organizations.

- I appreciate the ministry of the Center for Congregational Health at the Baptist Hospital in Winston-Salem, North Carolina, where I received my training as an Intentional Interim Minister and the use of the material in Appendix that introduces the Intentional Interim Ministry.
- A special thanks to Rod L. Reinecke and Ruth R. Wright, church consultants and trainers with ConTrOD Associates, who thoroughly read the manuscript and gave suggestions that made it more readable and useful. I appreciate permission to use their "Workable Problem Statement" at the end of Chapter 1.

I am greatly indebted to Speed B. Leas and Roy W. Pneuman for the use of their material and their reading of this manuscript and their feedback.

- Speed B. Leas, Senior Consultant of the Alban Institute, has researched and published widely in the area of church conflict. I appreciate the use of his "Five Levels of Church Conflict," used in Chapter 1. The use of his material should greatly benefit congregations.

- Roy W. Pneuman, Senior Consultant, Emeritus, with The Alban Institute granted permission to use his research and article on "Nine Common Sources of Conflict in Churches," included in Chapter 2, and also gave permission to include his "Source Checklist for Conflicted Congregations" as Appendix E.

- Thanks to Norris Smith, now retired from LifeWay Christian Resources of the Southern Baptist Convention (SBC), who introduced me to the helpful and insightful research project on "Forced Termination and Church Conflict."

- Thanks to Fred McGehee, Sr., Consultant in Pastoral Ministries, and Wayne Oakes, Consultant with Pastoral Ministries and Church Conflict at the Baptist State Convention of North Carolina for their encouragement and permission to use the "Commission on Ministry Report Survey of Forced Termination Questionnaire."

- One of the first congregations that I had the privilege to speak to following "my calling" into the ministry was at Bobby Stafford's home church. From the beginning he has been a supportive fellow minister. I appreciate his comments and suggestions concerning this book. I also commend him for the great job that he has done in encouraging and supporting congregations and church leaders in North Carolina as Senior Consultant for Associational Development at the North Carolina State Convention.

- Many thanks to John C. LaRue, Jr., Vice President of Online Services at www.ChristianityToday.com for permission to quote from his invaluable research published in *Your Church* magazine, a "Special Report on Forced Exits."

- Thanks to Leon Simpson, now a pastor in Ohio and formerly an editor at LifeWay Christian Resources of the SBC. His guidance in clear thinking and focused writing that benefit God's people has been most encouraging in the writing and formation of this book.

I am especially indebted to those who read, made suggestions and/or endorsed this writing project including:

- To D. James Kennedy, Senior Minister at Coral Ridge Presbyterian Church and President & Speaker of Coral Ridge Television and Radio Ministries in Fort Lauderdale, Florida.

- To the Honorable Mike Huckabee, Governor of Arkansas and former pastor and president of the Arkansas Baptist Convention, for the use of his quote found in the *Deacon* Magazine.

- To Kenneth Hemphill, author and President of Southwestern Baptist Theological Seminary in Ft. Worth, TX, for his endorsement.
- To Brain Harbour, pastor of First Baptist Church, Richardson, TX, and author of many books including a helpful preaching resource for pastors called *Brian's Lines.*

- To William H. Willimon, author and Dean of the Chapel and Professor of Christian Ministry at Duke University in Durham, NC, for his endorsement.

- I want to thank author: Gordon MacDonald, and also Louis McBurney, Director and Founder of the Marble Retreat in Marble Colorado for permission to quote from their material previously published in *Leadership.*

- I appreciate the wise counsel Alice Cullinan, head of the Religion Department at Gardner-Webb University, has given me as a former professor and co-worker on church staff. Her suggestions concerning this manuscript proved to be invaluable.

- To Rev. Terry Sharpe from Virginia who critiqued my manuscript and submitted helpful articles dealing with church conflict.

- To Bill Reynolds and Rev. Elwood C. Bredbenner with the Biblical Wellness Ministries in Raleigh, NC, who provided valuable feedback.

- To Ed McCann, a long-time friend and a deacon in the first church I served as pastor in Roseland, VA, for his endorsement.

- I appreciate permission to use cartoons by Jonny Hawkins and Joseph Farris. Thanks, guys, for encouraging us to laugh at ourselves. That is always helpful in managing conflict.

Thanks to those authors and trainers listed in the Endnotes and the additional resource Appendices for the guidance provided in their writings and training.

Author Jess Liar once said, "Everyone needs five shining faces." Faces that we can call on, depend upon and turn to for love, encouragement and friendship. I am so blessed to have those shining faces in my family: Pam, Nathan and Rachael, and those to whom I have ministered with and ministered to certainly make up a larger tribe than five. I am thankful.

If you have contributed to the making of this book and I have forgotten to mention you, please forgive me and know that your help with this project has certainly contributed to its success of being published.

Jesus said, "Without me you can do nothing." He is certainly a "shining face," and a friend who is closer than a brother. And is it not true that without one another we can do nothing? The truth is, we need each other—not just to write books, but to live and to make life more interesting and more fulfilling. And then when the storms of conflict blow our way, we'll have friends and strong relationships that will encourage and sustain us until the storm passes by.

To each of you, thanks!

TABLE OF CONTENTS

INTRODUCTION

"Churches are using termination as the 'weapon of choice' in targeting church staff problems in epidemic proportions," said Rev. Mike Huckabee, Governor of Arkansas and former pastor and President of the Arkansas Baptist Convention, in *The Deacon* magazine.[1]

Norris Smith, Forced Termination Consultant for LifeWay Church Resources of the Southern Baptist Convention, stated that a 1998 survey showed that more than 77 Southern Baptist pastors are fired each month.[2]

Edward B. Bratcher, author of *The Walk-On-Water Syndrome,* related a story at a pastors' conference that sadly supports the previous statements by Huckabee and Smith. He said a pastor friend conducted an experiment at pastors' conferences. He would walk up to a stranger, put his arm around him, and say, "I heard what was going on in your church, and I just want you to know that I'll be praying for you." Invariably every pastor would respond by saying, "How did you know?" A humorous, but enlightening experiment and a very sad commentary on the spiritual and emotional health of many pastors and congregations.[3]

Instead of congregations being a refuge for the weary and broken-hearted, they too often have become war zones where pastors and congregations fight for their lives and become spiritually, emotionally and even physically wounded instead of healed. It is no wonder that church leaders and laypersons alike become so discouraged and disillusioned with the church and church fights that they become burned out and spiritually broken. Often the result is that pastors and church members leave the church for safer and more enjoyable interests. This is why this book, "*Pastor, We Need To Talk!,*" came to be written. It is hoped that these suggestions and preventives will provide strategies to help the congregation and the pastor talk about their problems before a major conflict threatens the congregation's witness and ministry.

I have written this book out of a passion to help congregations, church staff and ministers who are hurting. Just as a person with pneumonia cannot run a marathon, so a congregation cannot accomplish The Great Commission if it is in unmanaged conflict.

A church fight and split is much like many divorces where nobody wins. Granted, there are cases where pastors and other church staff persons should move on, but even termination should be accomplished in a humane, Christ-like, and professional manner. No matter who is at fault in the conflict, the pastor, the church staff, and the congregation will all suffer if the conflict isn't addressed promptly and responsibly.

Regardless of how the conflict developed, termination of the pastor should never be the first option. (The use of "pastor" in this book is meant to include all staff, male and female. The pronoun "he" will be used, instead of he/she, with the knowledge that there is an increase in the number of females entering the pastoral ministry in various denominations.)

This book is a plea for congregations to recall the encouraging and warning words the Apostle Paul speaks to the church at Ephesus:

> Put on the full armor of God, that you may be able to stand firm against the schemes of the devil. For our struggle is not against flesh and blood, but against the rulers, against the powers, against the world forces of

this darkness, against the spiritual forces of wickedness in the heavenly places, " (Eph.6:11-12).

Too often the church spends its time fighting assumed enemies and wounding its own soldiers. Instead of being Christian soldiers marching on to Zion, they spend their time fighting each other. Any time a congregation fights or a congregation splits, it is a sign that someone did not get his or her way. Churches are to grow and multiply by evangelism, not by division. Is it not evident that Satan does not want the "Body of Christ" to be unified? Jesus stated Satan's desire for the church when He said, "The thief comes only to steal, and kill, and destroy...." (Jn.10:10a).

. The local church family accomplishes much in spite of itself, but how much more effective, Christ-like, and productive in God's work congregations could be if they were unified, focused and determined to love, forgive and work together for the cause of Christ. But unity comes at a price. It will require that all members of a congregation become more Christ-like in attitude and behavior toward their brothers and sisters.

Unity in the "Body of Christ" must not be claimed at any cost, but it must be pursued for congregations to function as healthy, helpful, "Christ-like" organizations.

Unity in the "Body of Christ" must not be claimed at any cost, but it must be pursued for congregations to function as healthy, helpful, "Christ-like" organizations.

The apostle Paul begs the church at Ephesus to preserve unity. He says:

"I THEREFORE, the prisoner of the Lord, entreat you to walk in a manner worthy of the calling with which you have been called, with all humility and gentleness, with patience, showing forbearance to one another in love, being diligent to preserve the unity of the Spirit in the bond of peace" (Eph.4:1-3).

Unity in any congregation doesn't just happen. Members must persistently work for unity with humility, gentleness, patience and love. As my long-time friend Dr. Paul Sorrells says, "It's hard to knock a person down when you have your arm around him." This book is a call and challenge for congregations not to try to avoid conflict, (which is inevitable), but to work through conflict and learn that unity in the church can be preserved and fellow Christians can be supported and encouraged in the work that God has called each to do.

It is my prayer that you will find in this book a reason and the encouragement to seek alternatives to terminating your pastor and church staff.

Dennis J. Hester
Winston-Salem, NC

Author's Note

If a significant number of members in your church are eager to fire your pastor or a staff member, you probably will not benefit from reading this book. However, if you are searching for "Christ-like" alternatives to terminating your pastor or a staff member – read on!

Cartoon used by permission from cartoonist Jonny Hawkins[4]

1

"At what level or stage of conflict is your congregation?"

Johnny's mother seemed to be consumed with ironing crisp white sheets, but little did Johnny know that even while ironing, she was preoccupied with thinking about him. He was six years old and had yet to speak his first word.

On this particular day, while Johnny sat silently playing and watching his mother, the telephone rang. She had only been on the phone for about a minute when Johnny screamed, "Fire! Fire! Mommy, the sheets are on fire!" Johnny's mother came running into the smoke-filled room, and in the midst of fanning the smoke from the room, she stopped, turned to Johnny with a bewildered look, and said, "Johnny, you can talk! You can really talk. Why haven't you said anything until today?"

With a little boyish grin Johnny looked up at his mother and said, "Well, up till now everything's been running pretty smoothly."

This story is typical of many congregations. Things run pretty smoothly for a while and then things begin to heat up. Many parishioners and staff members can smell the smoke and often see the flames about to engulf their harmonious fellowship, but, unlike little Johnny, no one says anything. No one wants to talk about the fire, the conflict that is threatening the congregation's health, witness and ministry.

No church can escape conflict. And the way the members and the pastor respond determines the church's witness and ministry in the future.

Many pastors respond to conflict by denial and relocation. They may think, "If I avoid the conflict, it will miraculously go away," or "If I pray enough, God will resolve the whole issue." To get out of a painful situation the pastor often simply begins to circulate his resume in the hope of moving before it gets any "hotter." Relocating, if possible, is a way to withdraw quickly from the conflict and avoid the pain.

Although the most common way congregations respond to conflict is to fire the pastor, another way is for congregations to become "cold" toward their pastor. As the conflict becomes more painful, members begin to distance themselves from the pastor, avoiding him, not responding to his leadership, and not allowing him to minister to them.

A former Director of Missions stated that at least five ministers came to his office every week, some of them weeping, saying, "Please help me find another church. I'll go anywhere, just get me out of the situation I'm in." The "situation" the pastors were referring to usually involved conflict.

Many pastors respond to conflict by denial and relocation. Many congregations respond to conflict by firing the pastor or becoming "cold" toward him and his leadership.

There are options for the pastor other than relocation. If he does not resolve some personal issues, he may infect his next congregation with the bitterness and resentment he carries with him.

There are other options for the congregation. Often problems can be worked out if conflict management strategies are used. One of the first strategies in resolving or managing conflict is to determine the level of conflict that the church is experiencing. By determining the level of conflict, members will be better able to determine: (1) how serious the present conflict is, (2) if the conflict is growing, (3) what can be done to manage or resolve the conflict, and (4) if outside help is needed to resolve the conflict.

Speed B. Leas, a Senior Consultant of the Alban Institute, is an expert in conflict management, development of volunteer programs, leadership development and management skills. In *Moving Your Church Through Conflict*, Leas identifies five levels of conflict. In the following paragraphs the levels of conflict are briefly described by incorporating Leas' description of each level of conflict. This brief description does not do Leas' book justice, but it will at least acquaint you with these five stages.

When the word "parties" is used, it refers to the pastor, the congregation and congregational members. The word "problem" is synonymous with the word "conflict." As you think about your church and the level of conflict you are experiencing, please note that Leas reminds us that both parties do not have to be at the same level.

Level One: Problem to Solve

At the first level of conflict Leas states that all parties in the congregation understand they have a "real disagreement" going on that involves conflicting goals, values, needs, etc. They believe the disagreement can be resolved and are willing to work with each other to find a solution to their problem.

Anger is short-lived and quickly controlled, but each party may begin to feel uncomfortable in the presence of the other. However, the focus is on the problem rather than the other persons involved in the disagreement. There is open sharing of information about the facts surrounding the conflict. Language is clear, precise and direct.

At this level of conflict all parties involved are working for a solution. Both parties should be able to walk away from the "negotiation table" feeling good. At this level both parties, to some degree, get what they want. This is called a win/win resolution.

Level Two: Disagreement

At this level of conflict all parties understand they have a real disagreement, states Leas. As in **Level One**, the anger is short-lived and quickly controlled, but the parties begin to focus on the other people involved rather than on solving the problem.

The conflict is becoming more intense because there is the beginning of distrust between the groups. Parties begin to talk about "them," and "those people," as opposed to "us."

Shrewdness and calculation to win is seen in one or both parties. Information is withheld, and hostile humor, barbed comments, and put-downs are commonly heard.

Leas says that at this level people want to protect themselves and come out of the conflict "looking good," and that it takes more effort at this level for the parties involved to find a win/win resolution to their conflict.

Level Three: Contest

When parties get to this level and beyond, they are in serious trouble, and Leas believes that an outsider is needed: a church consultant or mediator with advanced mediation skills.

Parties begin to develop a win/lose attitude. The pastor and the congregation begin to attack each other verbally. Church members begin to take sides and threaten to leave the church. Information is grossly distorted and only shared with "someone in the group." People speak in overgeneralizations, such as "You always. . . and "We never. . . ." The conflicted groups now want to win regardless of the cost.

The heart of this book will be most beneficial where church conflict does not exceed Levels One or Two (in some instances, Level Three). Beyond this Level people will find it difficult to heed these suggestions.

Level Four: Fight or Flight

At this level the conflicted parties shift from wanting to win to wanting to get rid of a person. A clear line has been drawn in the sand. Opposing parties have now become identifiable solid groups. They no longer believe others can change or want to change. Parties become cold and self-righteous and will not speak to the opposing party and will not listen to a different opinion.

Leas states that people now begin to use personal "church or religious language" instead of talking about the issue. Members of each party believe they know God's will or the moral and spiritual thing to do. Issues become "black and white" with little gray and room for flexibility. People see the conflict in one way—their way. Anyone who disagrees with them is definitely wrong.

The conflicted parties' goals at this level are no longer winning, but elimination. The parties want to "get rid of" or at least hurt the other person or parties. This is the result of those involved in the conflict who want to "fight."

Others will choose the option of "flight" by withdrawing their resources, money, time and talent, or even leaving the church. This may cause a congregational split.

Level Five: Intractable

(Controlling, Rebellious and Unmanageable)

At this level of conflict it may be necessary to "call 911!"

When pastors and congregations get to this level of conflict, they no longer have any understanding of the issue(s);

personalities have become the issue. The conflict has become unmanageable. "There is a relentless obsession of the parties to accomplish their goals at all costs," states Leas.

At this level the pastor and the congregation are out to hurt each other. The congregation works not only to get rid of their pastor, but also to see that he never serves another church as pastor. The pastor too can be vindictive and can try to harm the church's reputation in the hope that the church will find it difficult to find another pastor.

There is no objectivity or control of emotions in the conflicted groups. The other party is seen as evil and harmful, not only to the church, but also to society. The language used by persons in each opposing party reveals that their objective is to destroy the other party.

The outcome at this level of conflict is highly destructive. It may be necessary to physically remove members from the building or take legal steps in order to make the church a safe place. At this point, some denominations would have someone come in and help administer the church so that the congregation can continue to function.

Level Zero: Suppression/Denial or Post-Traumatic Stress

Recently Leas has added another level to his pyramid of conflict. If you recall, at **Level Five** the conflict in a congregation has become unmanageable and the focus is now on the elimination and/or destruction of the other. But what happens after the physical and verbal battle "appears to have ended" is just as painful and damaging to the life, ministry and witness of the war-torn congregation.

Leas says that after a congregation has experienced a conflict at Level Five the congregation will experience a state of shock or what is known as Post-Traumatic Stress. There will be a suppression and denial of feelings. Members will not allow themselves to talk about what has happened. They fear that to bring up the history of the church will only force them to re-live the painful feelings they have now so cleverly denied.

John Savage, an ordained United Methodist minister and president of L.E.A.D. Consultants, a leadership, education, and development training firm, agrees that the pain and the memories are still there deep in the hearts and minds of the congregation. It's very easy for the congregation, as it is for an individual, to "seal off pain" by suppressing the memories and refusing to talk about what brought the congregation so much embarrassment and hurt. Just like an individual, if the congregation refuses to "deal with their painful history," it will become "hard hearted," cold, indifferent and non-responsive.

Just like an individual, if the congregation refuses to "deal with their painful history," it will become "hard hearted," cold, indifferent and non-responsive.

Think about it. The pastor and congregation that once warned others about the dangers and horrors of hell have now experienced a hell of their own: a civil war if you will. Brother and sister have fought against each other. They can recall the glaring eyes, the red faces, the clinched fists. They can still hear the sharp, angry words of resentment and jealous and bitter competition that possessed church staff and laypersons alike to say and do things that surprised and embarrassed one another. No wonder they are in shock. Visitors walk into their worship service on Sunday morning and there is a deathly quietness. They are cold, lifeless and unresponsive. There are few signs of love, peace and joy. When they sing, "Victory in Jesus," they sound more like victims instead of victorious Christians. Even though they may talk with one another, there is a coolness, a distance and an obvious effort to be cautious as they relate to one another. These are the signs of a hurting, wounded congregation. They are experiencing a deep grief because they have experienced a great loss. Some of them lost a pastor or staff person whom they supported and loved. Church members are now gone and show no signs of returning. The church has lost its innocence. Why are members not talking about this horrendous battle that shocked their congregation and community? They are in shock, and they would rather deny what has gone on in the past few months because it simply hurts too much to talk about it. Instead of dealing with their past by reflecting, confessing, forgiving and learning from their conflict, they would rather deny that anything ever happened—especially if they are guilty of contributing to the conflict.

If the congregation can admit and come to terms with its history, the good, the bad and the ugly, it increases the chances of being a healthy, effective and productive congregation.

If the congregation can admit and come to terms with its history, the good, the bad and the ugly, it increases the chances of being a healthy, effective and productive congregation.

Organizations such as The Alban Institute, The Center for Congregational Health and Dr. John Savage with LEAD Consultants (see appendix for contact information) specialize in helping churches work through their painful history, and effect healing and a refocusing of energy.

Leas says: "The simplest way to manage conflict is to keep difference of opinion at **Level One**, or to move the people to **Level One** so that everyone can see and agree that 'we have a problem to solve.'" One way to accomplish this is to write "Workable Problem Statements." The statements should be

- free of blame
- specific and descriptive
- not related to the distant past
- not a "put-down" of any involved parties
- agreed to by all involved as a definition of problem [1]

You may find the "Problem Solving/Decision Making Process," used by church consultants, Rod L. Reinecke and Ruth Wright of ConTrOD Associates helpful.

Parties who have a conflict or disagreement may discuss the following items:

1. **What are we trying to decide?**
   Be sure this is clear to everyone.
   HOW will we decide?
   What methods or procedures will we use? (Consensus or Voting?)
   Deal with one issue at a time.
   Define the problem in a way everyone can accept.

2. **What alternatives do we have?**
   Consider as many as possible—brainstorm—don't evaluate yet.
   LISTEN to other viewpoints.
   Show that you **HEAR** and **UNDERSTAND** even when you don't agree.
   Share your feelings about the issues as well as your ideas.

3. **How might each alternative work?**

4. **Which alternative or combination of alternatives should we choose?**

5. **What do we need to do to carry out the decision?**

6. **Who will do what by when?** (Be specific).

7. **When and how will we evaluate?** [2]

In addition to understanding the levels of conflict a congregation needs to know the causes of conflict. Although there are many causes of conflict, the nine discussed in the next chapter are some of the most common.

2

Do you know the sources of your conflict?

Why do congregations and pastors get into trouble? According to Roy W. Pneuman, Senior Consultant Emeritus of the Alban Institute, there are nine common sources of conflict in churches. [1] (See Pneuman's Checklist located in the Appendices that complements Pneuman's list in this chapter).

Following each source of conflict that Pneuman identifies, the author suggests a way to prevent this type of conflict in the future.

1. People disagree about values and beliefs.

"Members do not agree about the church's nature, mission, goals or objectives," says Pneuman.

Suggestion:

Congregations need to develop a mission statement that is widely owned and embraced, and will clarify values and beliefs. When a congregation understands its purpose and goals, members tend to work together with less conflict.

2. The structure is unclear.

There are no clear guidelines about the roles and responsibilities of ministers, staff, laypersons or committees.

Pneuman notes: "No one is sure who is to do what; therefore people challenge anything anybody tries to do."

Suggestions:

Write job descriptions for every staff person, every committee and every organization in the church. Review and update when needed. Share this information openly and freely with the congregation.

3. There is conflict over the pastor's role and responsibilities.

There is a lack of agreement between pastor and congregation about what activities should be the pastor's priority.

Suggestions:

Pastors may boast, "God is my boss, not the church. I do what God tells me to do." When pastors or congregations become controllers "in the name of God," there will be conflict. Consensus is the key. Neither pastor nor congregation can get 100% of what they want, and neither can they give 100% of what the other party needs. Written surveys and sharing sessions can determine the priorities of both parties.

4. The structure no longer fits the congregation's size.

Here Pneuman reminds us that congregations often change in size. The expectations and responsibilities of the pastor and congregation must change accordingly.

Arlin J. Rothauge's small booklet, *Sizing Up A Congregation for New Member Ministry,* assigns four categories of size: small, medium, large, and extra large. Rothauge states that understanding the different sizes "prevents us from using one program and one style of leadership for all church situations." He adds that "the size of a congregation acts as a key variable in those factors that determine the structure, functions, and style of relationships in its group life."

Rothauge's research and observations answer five questions that should interest congregations and pastors:

- What is the basic structure of each type of church: family, pastoral, program, and corporate?
- How does each category typically attract new members?
- What are the predominant characteristics of entry of the new member?
- What are the basic needs of the new member in each size congregation?
- How might a church most effectively meet those basic needs of a new member?

It would benefit a congregation and pastor to read and study Rothauge's booklet in order to understand a changing congregation. [2]

Roy M. Oswald in his book, *Making Your Church More Inviting,* echoes Rothauge's theory of congregational size and pastoral leadership. Oswald says that "whether churches are growing or downsizing, congregations hold on to deeply engrained assumptions about what constitutes a dynamic church and what effective clergy do. The inflexibility of these expectations is an important cause of clergy malfunctioning." [3]

Following are the four sizes of congregations identified by Rothauge.

THE FAMILY CHURCH
0-50 ACTIVE MEMBERS
Usual Context: Rural Areas, some Urban Centers, and Small Towns

"What Family Churches want from clergy is pastoral care," says Oswald. "Clergy are to be the chaplain of this small family which is controlled by patriarchs and matriarchs."

THE PASTORAL CHURCH
50 – 150 ACTIVE MEMBERS
Usual Context: Towns and Suburbia

Oswald reminds us that unlike The Family Church, clergy is usually at the center of a Pastoral Church. Usually a seminary-trained pastor and trained lay leaders replace the patriarchs and matriarchs. Keys to success in The Pastoral Church are open communication between staff and lay persons and the pastor's ability to delegate, assign responsibilities and affirm the accomplishments of others. Without these changes in leadership the whole congregation will become weakened; the pastor will experience burnout and the congregation's fellowship, productivity and unity will degenerate.

THE PROGRAM CHURCH
150 – 350 ACTIVE MEMBERS
Usual Context: Larger Towns, Urban and Growing Suburban Areas

In The Program Church there is an even greater need for pastors, staff and laypersons to be trained and to work as a team. Programs are highly emphasized with lay leaders taking on "pastoral-type functions." The pastor acts much like a coach: recruiting, training, supervising, evaluating and motivating congregational leaders.

"Unless the pastor gives high priority to the spiritual and pastoral needs of lay leaders, those programs will suffer," says Oswald.

THE CORPORATION CHURCH
(also called by others a Corporate or Resource Church)
350 - 500+ ACTIVE MEMBERS
Usual Context: Cities and Metropolitan Areas

In this size church, Oswald says that the congregation's close relationship with senior pastors is willingly sacrificed in favor of the Corporate Church's variety and quality of programs. The make-up of these churches is complex, and the pastor becomes a symbol of unity, stability and motivation for the congregation. The pastor is usually a multi-skilled person with emphasis on leadership more than management.

"While managers can manage the energy of a parish, leaders can *generate* energy," says Oswald. "The Corporate Church needs leaders who know how to build momentum. Otherwise, even when managed well, these large churches run out of gas and begin to decline."

In Summary:

When the congregation's size changes, the change doesn't feel good. It is an understatement to say that congregation and pastor must adjust to the re-sizing. Too often he and the congregation are aware that the size of their church has changed, but they are not aware that they have not changed their expectations of each other.

> ***"When a parish crosses the boundary between one size and another, it needs to begin relating to its clergy in fairly radically different ways than previously," says Oswald***

Oswald says, "Some of the greatest upheaval caused by numerical growth occurs when a congregation is on the border-line between two sizes." He goes on to say, "When a parish crosses the boundary between one size and another, it needs to begin relating to its clergy in fairly radically different ways than previously."

Too often, pastors are labeled as "bad" pastors when they are simply frustrated pastors because they are trying to function in a larger congregation than they are used to. Similarly, a pastor may feel unfulfilled because his congregation is declining. The congregation no longer demands as much administration and planning as it once did. And it's not because the congregation or the pastor is "bad;" it's because each is unaware that church size has changed.

Suggestions:

Congregations would do well to remember that the size of a congregation imposes unique challenges and limitations upon pastors. The bottom line for the pastor is to feel called to a certain size of congregation. The bottom line for the congregation is to call a suitable person for their size.

In essence, the question for each party is: “Are we a good match for each other?”

5. The pastor's leadership style is mismatched with the congregation.

Pneuman describes leadership style in terms of two dimensions: task and relationship.

Suggestions:

Some pastors are task-oriented. They enjoy administration, meetings, and the planning and leading that are necessary in a congregation. Other pastors are relations-oriented. They like to mingle with people, build relationships, and discover people's needs and minister to those needs. They enjoy visitation, counseling, pastoral care and activities that keep them close to the people.

The conflict comes when a congregation expects a pastor of one orientation to function in the other orientation. Please

> ***Conflict is reduced when a church takes the time to study what it needs in a pastor.***

recognize that both types of pastors are needed. Neither is better than the other. Some pastors even have a good mix of both skills. A congregation needs both skills. But usually pastors have a dominant style of leadership—either in task or relationship. Oftentimes congregations will hire additional staff or use lay leadership to complement the leadership abilities of the pastor. Conflict is reduced when a church takes the time to study what it needs in a pastor. (See the Appendix J concerning the Intentional Interim Ministry).

Conflict is also reduced when pastors intentionally and appropriately "try" to integrate, like Jesus did, a task/goal and a people/relationship style of leadership.

Concerning these two orientations of leadership, Harris W. Lee, author of *Effective Church Leadership* asks:

> Which is best? Which is most suitable and effective for work in the church? When we consider the ministry of Jesus we realize that we need both orientations. Jesus' message, of course, was one of high relationships. He attracted the masses; he exhibited grace and compassion; he said, "This I command you, to love one another" (John 15:17). In another sense, Jesus was task-oriented, concerned about the accomplishment of his Father's work: "I glorified thee on earth, having accomplished the work which thou gavest me to do" (John 17:4). He seemed driven to his task: "We must work the works of him who sent me, while it is day; night comes when no man can work" (John 9:4). His exhortation to his followers was one of work: "Go therefore and make disciples of all nations, baptizing. . . and teaching. . . " (Matt.28:19, 20).

> Jesus was able to integrate the two orientations; he could be effectively task-oriented or person-oriented according to the situation at hand and his purpose at the time." [4]

Before you continue with Pneuman's nine common sources of conflict, look at the Typical Pastor Profile (next page) and identify your style or your pastor's style of leadership.

6. A new pastor rushes into changes.

Pneuman states, "Many new pastors do not take the time and trouble necessary to get to know the congregation before making changes."

Suggestions:

Pastors often say, "The seven words of a dying church are 'we never did it this way before.'" It is true many churches are stuck in tradition. To try to change the time of offering in the worship service, how the Lord's Supper is conducted, or how church officers are elected would be enough to cause a major conflict for a newly elected pastor.

Churches say they want leadership from the new pastor, but often they mean "not right away." Pastors must pay the price of committing themselves to serve the Lord in one congregation long enough to build substantial relationships and trust before they can make significant changes in the life of a congregation. Congregations and pastors must work as a team and enlist the support of one another in decision-making and goal setting. The ministry should not be a "Lone Ranger" task, either for the pastor or the congregation.

Typical Pastor Profile

Ask your congregation, "What type of Pastor do we need?")

Task/Goal Type Pastor	Relationship Type Pastor
1. Stresses importance of goal-setting 2. Enjoys completing goals and projects 3. Enjoys building buildings, starting new programs and ministries 4. Spends time in the church office 5. Enjoys administration, planning, meetings and helping the church accomplish its goals and vision	1. Stresses building personal relationships 2. Enjoys ministering to individuals 3. Enjoys coaching /building people, helping them to grow in their faith 4. Likes being in the community visiting 5. Enjoys counseling, pastoral care and activities that require closeness to the people & ministering to needs.

A Reminder to Congregations:

- Neither the "Task" type nor the "Relationship" type pastor is bad - only different.
- One pastoral leadership type is not better than the other.
- Congregations can benefit from both types of pastors.
- At different times in the life of a congregation the congregation may need one type of pastor more than the other type. The key to a long relationship is knowing the needs of the congregation and matching a pastoral leadership type to the congregation.
- Congregations need some of both sets of skills in a pastor. When particular skills are lacking in a pastor, the members would do well to support their pastor in increasing skills that are lacking or hire additional staff.
- There are some pastors who have a good mix of skills that are both "Task" and Relationship" oriented.
- Conflict begins when a congregation tries to force one type of pastor to be the other type of pastor.

Created by Dennis J. Hester (Permission granted to copy)

7. Communication lines are blocked.

Pneuman sees poor communication not as the source of conflict but "more a result of conflict than a cause of conflict."

Suggestions:

"One hand must know what the other hand is doing." Secrets, murmuring, gossip, rumors about the congregation or the pastor can damage and destroy relationships, quench the Spirit, sow seeds of discontentment, and create so much disunity that a pastor and congregation can no longer have an effective ministry. A clear and continuous flow of information from the pulpit - in bulletins, newsletters, and meetings and in daily conversation - is essential to keep the lines of communication open. Likewise, lay leaders and members need to communicate their ideas, responses, thoughts and feelings.

8. Church people manage conflict poorly.

"People seem to believe that conflict is evil and that it shouldn't happen in the church," Pneuman observes. And as a result, "Even if conflict is there, we won't recognize it."

Suggestions:

According to the Apostle Paul, as long as Christians are in this world, they will be dealing with fleshly desires and impulses. Conflict is inevitable in human beings. One pastor told a couple who came for counseling, "The main problem with your marriage is that you both married sinners." If couples must recognize that biblical fact, so must churches. Churches must not be surprised when conflict comes. They can work through conflict and move on with a more effective ministry and witness to the community.

9. Disaffected members hold back participation and pledges.

When people are dissatisfied, they will vote with their feet and their money. Pneuman notes, "Unless the pastor is ministering to and listening to all segments of the congregation, sooner or later those who are not feeling heard will initiate a series of efforts to gain his attention. If these do not work, they may try power plays which may result in the pastor's departure."

Suggestions:

Once again, the pastor and the congregation must be brave enough to speak up and humble enough to hear the other party's opinion. Openness is the key.

Pneuman adds, "There's nothing in the list that can't be dealt with when the conflict is at the level of constructive disagreement.... Once any of these difficulties escalates to win-lose confrontation, it can be the dynamite that destroys healthy relationships..."

Based on Pneuman's list of Nine Common Sources of Conflict, I have devised a chart (on the following page) for you to record your church's sources and degrees of conflict.

I. D. Conflict

I. D. (Identify and Discuss) Your Sources of Conflict

Identify the issues that seem to be causing conflict in your church.	**RATE THE CONFLICT (1 to 5)** (Not to be confused with the level of conflict in Chapter 1) 1. Not a source of conflict 2. Potential source of conflict 3. Beginning of a conflict 4. A growing conflict 5. A major source of conflict	Why is this issue a conflict in your church?
1.		
2.		
3.		
4.		
5.		
6.		
7.		
8.		
Other:		

Created by Dennis J. Hester (Permission granted to copy)

3

How are you working for unity?"

"I THEREFORE, the prisoner of the Lord, entreat you to walk in a manner worthy of the calling with which you have been called, with all humility and gentleness, with patience, showing forbearance to one another in love, being diligent to preserve the unity of the Spirit in the bond of peace."
(Eph.4:1-3)

Church staff members shuffled their feet and squirmed in their pews, and the whole congregation exhaled a long dreadful sigh as Rev. Reeves announced his plans for a community-wide survey.

In a recent meeting the elders had explained to Rev. Reeves that the pastor before him, who had stayed for only 18 months, had almost split the church over the same issue. The elders explained that the congregation had expended a lot of time and money in such surveys with very little results.

One of the elders said to to the pastor during their meeting, "I'm not giving up another Sunday afternoon to have doors slammed in my face while trying to dig up information on people who don't want to come to our church in the first place." He emphatically added, "If everyone in our church feels the same way that I do about community surveys they would admit that their hearts are not in this project." The rest of the elders looked at one another, during the meeting, and nodded their heads in agreement. Rev. Reeves looked the elders in the eye and proclaimed like a prophet, "If this church wants to grow, I believe it has to be done now!"

During the last church council meeting, the church staff had also informed the pastor that the calendar was full with approaching holiday activities, an upcoming Sunday School training retreat and a youth fundraiser. One of the church council members tried to explain to him, "I don't see how we can get enough people involved to effectively carry out this survey in the fall of the year when everyone is already committed to several other worthy projects." Rev. Reeves, in a deep and determined voice, leaned forward and quoted Matthew 6:33, "But seek first His kingdom and His righteousness; and all these things shall be added to you." And then he added, "It sounds to me that some people need to get their priorities in order."

As weeks went by the congregation became more irritated and resentful of Rev. Reeve's insistence for the congregation to participate in the survey. He grew more determined that the survey was of the Lord and desperately needed. Then the survey forms were handed out following a morning Bible study. The pastor gave final instructions concerning the community survey in a lengthy pep-rally style. But to his amazement, following worship service he noticed several survey forms lying on the floor, under the pews and stuffed in the racks behind the hymnbooks. And even though it hurt terribly, it set Rev. Reeves to thinking when he over-heard an elderly couple talking in the vestibule. One said, "This is one pet project the pastor will have to do himself. Besides that, I am tired of contributing to things that I don't think this church should be involved in." And with a crumbled-up survey form in one hand, she raised her cane in the other hand and said, "And I don't care who knows it either."

Such scenarios are played out in churches every week. A church leader wanting one thing and a congregation wanting another. Often times both parties are right and sometimes both parties are wrong. It is sad that for some people, words like "compromise" and "negotiation" are foreign. Some say, "You can disagree with me and be wrong if you want to," or "It's either my way or the highway." Those who foster such attitudes are merely allowing disunity to grow.

When people become discouraged and "hardhearted," they may become "hardheaded" as well and refuse to work for unity

In Isaiah 6:9-10, the prophet Isaiah described a people who already had their minds made up. They could not perceive the truth because their hearts were hardened.

When people become discouraged and "hardhearted," they may become "hardheaded" as well and refuse to work for unity. Remember, people must *want* to communicate: to talk, to listen, and to understand a different point of view. Unity will not be accomplished until steps toward communication and understanding are taken.

Stephen Covey, best-selling author of *The 7 Habits of Highly Effective People,*[1] (Stephen R. Covey, 1989) says: "We have such a ten-dency to rush in, to fix things up with good advice. But we often fail to take the time to diagnose, to really, deeply understand the problem first."

If I were to summarize in one sentence the single most important principle I have learned in the field of interpersonal relations, it would be this: *seek first to understand, then to be understood.* This principle is the key to effective interpersonal communication."[1]

Consider these questions that work for unity.

1. Are you speaking in a conversational tone that doesn't imply you want to fight?
2. Are you polite, gracious, and willing to hear the other person out before you speak?
3. Are you trying to find a way to solve this problem or is your underlying agenda to fire someone?
4. Have you called in other resourceful people who can mediate this conflict?
5. Are you too angry to talk? Should you give yourself some time to think about what has happened before you speak?
6. Are you willing to admit your part in this conflict?
7. Do you want this issue to be resolved, or do you simply enjoy a good fight? Remember Apostle Paul's advice: "... being diligent to preserve the unity..." Eph.4:3).

Some more things to keep in mind as you seek to preserve unity:

1. When someone is on their "soapbox," say to him or her: "I want to hear more of what you have to say."
2. If you disagree with a person say, "We need your contribution. I don't share your view, but there may be others who do. I respect your opinion, but I also have a right to my opinion." (Note that this is very hard for people to say when they have never said this to members of their own family).
3. Value other persons and their differences.
4. LISTEN! LISTEN! LISTEN!
   Savage, in his book, *Listening & Caring Skills, "A Guide for Groups and Leaders,"* says that "listening skills will enhance your own life and give you a chance to minister in a wonderfully new and healing way." He goes on to say, "Being an effective listener is one of the greatest gifts you can ever give to another." [2]
5. Let other persons know that their contributions really count.

6. If the underlying conflict isn't dealt with, there's a danger of premature healing from the outside in.
7. It is a myth that "we can solve everything." Some conflict cannot be resolved, but only managed.
8. Jesus was born in the midst of conflict, and throughout much of His life he dealt with conflicted situations. Luke 2:34 says, "... Behold, this Child is appointed for the fall and rise of many in Israel, and for a sign to be opposed." Jesus told His disciples, "Do not think that I came to bring peace on the earth; I did not come to bring peace, but a sword," (Mt.10:34).

An outsider looks in and sees – can you?

Rev. William's charisma brought into the church younger families that would fully support him. Therefore, Rev. Williams realized anything he wanted, he could get. He would often overhear one of the older "traditionalist minded members" saying, "The preacher is going to try to get approval for this new building fund with the help of his 'fan club,' but I am not going to give one penny to support something I don't feel the congregation is ready for, regardless of who favors the preacher. If the preacher wants to favor these people over those of us who founded the church, let them pay for 'his' new building."

"How are you working for unity?"

"A fool always loses his temper, but a wise man holds it back." (Pro. 29:11)

"So then each on of us shall give account of himself to God." (Rom. 14:12)

4

"Are you trying to solve a problem or get rid of a person?"

"Come now and let us reason together.
(Isa. 1:18).

"... build up one another... admonish the unruly Encourage the faint hearted, help the weak, be patient with all men," (I Thess.5:11,14).

"If we could just get rid of Rev. Jones, our problems would be over." This is the attitude of many congregations during **Level Four** conflict. Congregations and ministers alike may be like the person who says, "My job is fine. It's people who drive me crazy. If I didn't have to work with people I'd be all right." Unfortunately neither people nor problems will fade away, thus removing our responsibility of learning to deal with both of them.

In Gen. 4:1-5 a bitter sibling conflict occurred between Cain and Abel. Abel's offering to God was accepted. Jealousy, pride and envy filled Cain's heart because God rejected his offering. Cain's bitterness burned within him and drove him to kill his own brother.

Cain eliminated what he assumed to be his problem by killing his brother. The object of his resentment and jealousy was gone—but so was his brother.

If the pastor is terminated, a greater issue may remain. How will the congregation relate to the next pastor when a conflict occurs? Will the congregation immediately eliminate the new pastor as a "troublemaker?" Maybe the problem is deeper than the minister.

Termination is really the easy way out. The congregation might think that termination is less painful than working through conflict, but members seldom consider the "fallout" that occurs, and the toll it takes on the pastor and the church when a pastor is fired.

Consider the following additional problems that can occur when a pastor is terminated:

1. The purpose and mission of the congregation is de-focused.
2. There are embarrassments, hurt feelings, and seething anger that may explode at an inappropriate time. After all, at one time a majority of the congregation voted favorably to accept the pastor. There are usually quite a few members who still favor him even after termination.
3. The joy and morale of the congregation will plummet.
4. A minister's reputation is damaged.
5. The congregation's witness in the community is damaged.
6. Prospective candidates may be wary when they learn the previous pastor was terminated.
7. The congregation may be liable for a lawsuit.

To say that termination profoundly affects pastors, their families and their congregations is an understatement. John C. LaRue, Jr., Vice President of ChristianityToday.com, Christianity

"A church that regularly terminates pastors, that may develop a 'lifestyle of conflict' and create a pattern of unrest," says Dale.

Today International, conducted a nation-wide study in 1996 for *YOUR CHURCH* magazine whereby 999 randomly selected U.S. pastors who subscribe *to LEADERSHIP, CHRISTIANITY TODAY,* and *YOUR CHURCH,* were surveyed. This survey entitled, "Forced Exits," was published in five articles from May 1996 to February 1997. A total of 593 pastors responded to the survey, giving a 59 percent response rate. Following are a few facts that resulted from the survey. In the special report entitled, "Forced Exits: Personal Effects," LaRue found that:

> . . .following a forced exit, three-fourths of pastoral families had to move to a new residence. Two-thirds reported that their children had to change schools. And nearly two-thirds (64%) of pastors' spouses had to change jobs. In addition to the geographical and career changes, internal turmoils also made an impact. Nearly six out of ten (58%) experienced a drop in their confidence as a leader. Most pastors (54%) reported a heavy emotional toll on their spouse, and six out of ten said their family's ability to trust church leadership was undermined. In addition, a surprising one in ten pastors experienced a major illness within 12 months of being forced out. [1]

LaRue also found that approximately four out of every ten who had been forced out had not yet returned to pastoral ministry.

Robert D. Dale of the Center for Creative Church Leadership Development in Richmond, Virginia, makes a statement that reveals that churches are also profoundly affected when they terminate a pastor. He says, concerning a church that has regularly terminated pastors, that "The congregation may develop a 'lifestyle of conflict' and create a pattern of unrest."

LaRue's survey seems to support Dale's statement. LaRue says in his Special Report, entitled "Forced Exits: High-Risk Churches":

> The majority of ousted pastors (62%) were forced out by a church that had already forced out one or more pastors in the past. At least 15 percent of all U.S. churches fall into this category, having forced out two or more pastors. On average, these churches have forced out three to four pastors."

Most alarming, says LaRue:

> Ten percent of all U.S. churches, having forced out three or more pastors, can be called repeat offenders. These are the churches most likely to force out the next pastor that comes along. [2]

Many pastors are doomed from the day they join a congregation because the congregation's expectations are unachievable by any human being," says

Many churches choose firing because firing can be fast. Imagine hearing a church leader say, "Pastor, this coming Sunday will be your last worship service with us. Here's your check." In some Protestant denominations a Pastor Search Committee can be selected and searching for a new pastor within a few weeks. In a few more weeks, a new pastor can be elected, and the church will continue with "business as usual." But what about the problems the church encountered with the last pastor? Was anything resolved? Did the church learn anything? Did the pastor learn anything? What precautions have been taken that will increase the chances of this not happening again?

Too often, ministers become "scapegoats" for a congregation that isn't brave enough to admit its own mistakes or not willing enough to examine its job descriptions and expectations, which are often very unrealistic. George Barna writes in *Today's Pastors* that:

> many pastors are doomed from the day they join a congregation because the congregation's expectations are unachievable by any human being. No matter how skilled, how loving, how intelligent or how experienced the pastor might be, the people of the church expect too much too quickly for the pastor to have much chance of succeeding in their eyes. [3]

Congregations would do well to be patient with staff, be perceptive concerning their problems, and plan to deal with and learn from conflicts. Robert D. Dale in his book, *Pastoral Leadership*, says:

> Healthy congregations settle their differences promptly. By dealing with their conflicts more often, they use their ongoing experiences to learn how to resolve their fusses more constructively. [4]

If the congregation doesn't deal with the previous conflict, church leaders may soon be saying, "It looks like this minister has the same problem that the last minister had. I guess we need to get rid of him also." And the sad, painful pattern continues.

In Eph.5:21, (NIV) the Apostle Paul commands church members to "be subject to one another out of reverence for Christ." To do this, a congregation must develop an attitude of humility. The congregation must see itself as God's family, joined together and worthy of His love and forgiveness. To revere Christ is to respect and hold in highest regard anyone who claims the Name of Christ.

In actuality, the church needs and depends upon each member for safety, care, love, and encouragement. If members submit to one another, they must listen to one another, be challenged, and even corrected. They must understand that God speaks through the congregation as well as the pastor. The shepherd needs the sheep. The sheep need a shepherd. And with love and respect for each other, the pastor and the congregation can produce a wonderful ministry committed to "The Good Shepherd."

Too often, ministers become "scape-goats" for a congregation that isn't brave enough to admit its own mistakes

Ministers must not allow themselves to become offended when a member points out areas that need improvement. Church leaders must not become critical, defensive and unwilling to work to change when the minister or members make suggestions.

Today's society has become a "throw away" society. Ministers and congregations must not forget that people are fragile and hard to replace.

Will you be honest and answer these questions?

1. Has the conflict become personal? (The issue has become secondary. The primary "solution" is for the minister to leave.)
2. Are you more concerned about winning the fight than solving the problem?
3. Do you hear language such as, "*He or she* is the problem," instead of hearing, "*We* have a problem to solve?"
4. Are you tired of fighting, have you

God speaks through the congregation as well as the pastor.

run out of options, or just want the problem solved—even if it means firing someone?

5. Are you taking the easy way out?
6. Are you willing to communicate with others involved, or are you already distancing yourself from them? Remember that the gospel enables us to build bridges to one another instead of building walls that separate us from one another.
8. Are you praying, sharing and working together or politicking, scheming and working behind the scenes to "out maneuver" and get rid of the others involved?

An outsider looks in and sees — can you?

The business meeting was over, but out in the parking lot the conversation still revolved around what some interpreted as Rev. Jones' lack of respect for others' time. He was always late for meetings. And he had preached past twelve o'clock for the past three Sundays. (Several people were keeping count). It was time something was done. It was obvious that he was insensitive to his parishioners' schedules. But it seemed doubtful that Pastor Jones would change. He always said, "God has His own time clock." He was so "holy" and so authoritative that the congregation felt that to confront him would be almost like confronting God. No one knew why he had developed such a bad habit of ignoring others' time. The group in the parking lot had discussed this matter many times. They felt it would be less embarrassing and painful for everyone if they privately asked the pastor to leave. Then they could begin their search for a new pastor who would be more time-conscious.

Little did this small group realize that their behavior was not biblical nor was their manner of dealing with their dissatisfaction concerning their pastor's tardiness healthy or productive for the church body or for him.

Are you trying to solve a problem or get rid of a person?

"He has told you, O man, what is good.
And what does the LORD require of you,
But to do justice, to love kindness,
And to walk humbly with your God?"
(Mic. 6:8)

5

"Have you sought the will of God in this conflict?"

"Do nothing from selfishness or empty conceit, but with humility of mind let each of you regard one another as more important than himself; do not merely look out for your own personal interests, but also for the interests of others. Have this attitude yourselves, which was also in Christ Jesus." *(Phil.2:3-5)*

All Christians at one time or another may become "wounders" instead of "healers" and caregivers. Christians are sinners saved by grace and transformed into saints, but they may often act "in the flesh" instead of relating to others "in the spirit." In the story of the Good Samaritan (Luke 10:25-37), the Priest and the Levite (parallel to church leaders) passed by the "certain man in the ditch" who had a tremendous need. It's so easy to become emotional about the church building, a certain classroom or a memorial stained glass window and overlook people. Christ made people his priority.

The Apostle Paul exhorts Christians to look out for the interests of others, those who are hurting and have special needs (Phil.2:4). Jesus was forever showing His interest in how others felt.

Remember how sensitive Jesus was at the wedding feast in Cana? One reason he performed his first miracle was to spare the wedding couple and their guests the embarrassment of running out of good wine. Jesus was sensitive to others' feelings and the situations in which they found themselves.

The Apostle Paul exhorts us, "Have this attitude in yourselves which was also in Christ Jesus" (Phil.2:5).

In the midst of conflict, remember these principles:

1. Jesus' disciples were right where God wanted them to be when they found themselves in the midst of a terrible storm. "Teacher, do you not care that we are perishing?" asked His disciples (Mk.4:38). But they had failed to recall the promise of God: "I WILL NEVER DESERT YOU, NOR WILL I EVER FORSAKE YOU" (Heb.13:5).
   Even though your congregation is experiencing conflict, God knows where you are, and He is in the midst of your conflict.
2. Conflict may be one of the most creative, challenging times in the life of the church. So much can be learned, shared and "worked out" during this time.
3. You must never stop praying for God's people and God's pastor. God speaks through the congregation as well as the pastor. Therefore, everyone has a voice. And if the voices don't get too loud, God's voice may be heard—even in the conflict.
4. Please don't stop believing that God has a plan for your church. Jeremiah 29:11 says: "'For I know the plans that I have for you,' declares the LORD, 'plans for welfare and not for calamity to give you a future and a hope.'"

Isn't it pure joy to know that God has a plan for His church family in spite of the fact that members may sometimes act rudely toward one another?

Here are a few more suggestions in seeking the will of God:

1. Pray for unity, and pray for the person with whom you are at odds.
2. Our God is a God of order. Conflict is never his will, but learning from conflict is God's will.
3. A good question for the congregation to ask in the midst of conflict is: "What is God's message during this conflict? What does He want us to learn?

An outsider looks in and sees – can you?

The Pastor Search Committee had been very impressed with Rev. Haggard. Following a delicious covered-dish meal in the fellowship hall, he was meeting the congregation for the first time. He was very humble and seemed eager to hear what everyone had to say. So it wasn't surprising that he received a unanimous vote to become the pastor.

What was surprising was to hear Rev. Haggard stand in the pulpit three months later, stretch his arms wide, and proclaim, " I have been praying, and I believe God wants us to tear down this old sanctuary and build a new and larger building."

Two elderly ladies with eyes wide turned to each other, and one said, "That's strange, I've been praying also and God hasn't told me anything about a new building."

"I agree," whispered the other lady. "When Rev. Haggard first came, he was so eager to listen to our concerns. He was sensitive to what we felt God wanted us to do, but now it seems that he is the only one who can hear what God is saying. Doesn't he realize we serve the same God who talks to us also?"

"Have you sought the will of God in this conflict?

". . .let us pursue the things which make for peace and the building up of one another."
(Rom. 14:19)

6

"Are you treating every person as Christ would?"

"...be kind to one another, tender-hearted, forgiving each other, just as God in Christ also has forgiven you." (Eph.4:32)

I once asked a lady why she liked to watch "Judge Judy" on television. The lady smiled and responded, "Because every once-in-a-while I like to see someone else 'get what's coming to them.'" That sums up the feeling of a lot of people toward "wrong-doers." They believe people should pay and pay dearly for mistakes they've made. Christians often feel justified in judging and even enjoy majoring in retribution and judgment instead of mercy and grace.

Christ looked for every opportunity to give grace. To the woman caught in adultery, He asked, "Woman, where are they? Did no one condemn you?" And she said, "No one, Lord," And Jesus said, "Neither do I condemn you; go your way. From now on sin no more" (Jn.8:10-11).

Church members may treat those involved in conflict as would Jesus or as would Judge Judy. It's o.k. to be angry, but it's not o.k. to hurt people. Christians often have difficulty handling anger. Many people believe that the feeling of anger is a sin. But anger is just that—a feeling. People feel what they experience, whether it is anger or love. Anger is a normal human reaction to an embarrassing or painful experience. Anger is not an issue of right or wrong. How people respond when they become angry can become a moral issue, especially if they choose to retaliate.

Jesus cleared the temple with a whip (John 2:13-25). He must have been angry, but He chose not to hurt anyone physically, although He did hurt the moneychangers' pride and profits!

Anger is nothing more than a heightened 'cry for help,'" says Savage

Often when church members are angry and lash out for no apparent reason, there is some unresolved issue that is driving their behavior. They are trying to send a message. Savage says, "Anger is nothing more than a heightened 'cry for help.'" Those who are angry may feel they are being mistreated, or are embarrassed or not taken seriously. That's why it's important to discover what lies behind the anger that is being displayed, whether from pastor or people. What is the real issue that needs to be dealt with? Remember that anger is a "cry for help."

Common ways you can chose to handle anger during conflict:

1. **You can implode** (blowing up on the inside).
   You can deny your anger, hurt feelings and resentment. As the coach says, "Suck it up, boys. Just shake off the pain and let's go." To deny and "stuff" your pain is very damaging to your physical body, to your emotional health and to your spiritual well-being. You may eventually "implode," hurting yourself with guilt or harboring thoughts of hurting yourself. Emotional and physical illnesses often stem from unresolved anger.
2. **You can explode** (blowing up outwardly).

Sooner or later the anger that you deny or nurture will seep out: in a business meeting, during a difficult committee meeting, or at home where the pain can damage innocent victims. Nothing is more ugly than an Un-Christ-like Christian out of control.

3. **You can pout.**
   Pouting is a passive-aggressive behavior that keeps everyone at bay and keeps others guessing about why you are so irritable and seemingly so unhappy. Pouters don't talk. They mope around, and nobody knows why. It never dawns on many Christians to be biblical and honest about their anger.
4. **You can deal with your anger by gently and lovingly confronting the person with whom you are in conflict.**
   Jesus calls for you to be responsible in handling your anger. James Dobson, psychologist, author and host of "Focus on the Family" radio program, calls this behavior "tough love." "Tough love" allows you to confront in a gentle, Christ-like manner. It is often difficult, but if you love Christ, His Church and others, you must learn to deal with conflict appropriately "for Christ's sake." And you must love and respect yourself enough not to allow yourself to be mistreated—even if it is disguised in "church language" in the name of Jesus.

God's Word gives us some guidelines on how to handle conflict:

1. When someone hurts you, go directly to the person who caused the pain (Mt.5:22-25).
2. Forgive the person who offends you by using Jesus' "70 x 7" principle (Mt.18:21-35).
3. If the offender doesn't listen to you, ask the church leaders to talk with the offender (Mt.18:15-20).
4. Stay in control to magnify your witness (Jam.1:19-20).

5. Deal with anger or conflict within 24 hours, (Eph.4:26-27). Remember, delaying confrontation rarely resolves painful issues.
6. Remaining angry gives Satan an opportunity to kill, steal and destroy the unity in your congregation (Jn.10:10; II Cor.2:5-11).

   The late comedian and humorist Jerry Clower used to say, "I hope that I can act like a Christian in every situation."

An outsider looks in the church and sees - can you?

"It's obvious something is going on with Rev. Jackson. He has been rather irritable and has been preaching on hell for the past three Sundays," said Tom, one of the charter members of his church.

"Yes, that's true," responded his wife, Tammy. "He hasn't been the same since Deacon Lewis embarrassed him during the last church council meeting. And Deacon Lewis walks around red-faced, like a ticking time bomb. Someone should say something to both of them, but I'm afraid it may create WWIII right here in the church."

The couple gave a long sigh and almost simultaneously said, "Let's just pray the situation gets better before our Christmas cantata, since both men are narrators in the program. We surely don't want visitors seeing grown men acting this way."

Are you treating every person as Christ would?"

7

"Are you talking to each other in a way that can be understood?"

"... speaking the truth in love, we are to grow up in all aspects into Him, who is the head, even Christ,"

(Eph.4:15)

You may have heard someone say, "It's not what she said, it's the way that she said it." The way people say things can overpower what they mean, which leaves room for the wrong interpretation. This often leads to conflict. Church members must send messages in a manner that others will interpret correctly.

Yelling, retaliating and "getting in people's faces" will only keep a church fight going. If the pastor and people want to resolve conflict in a peaceful fashion, here are a few suggestions:

1. Begin all conflict resolutions with prayer and some ground rules that provide a safe place for open, honest discussion, free of judgment.

- Why pray? God is concerned about His people and His church. Praying is a reminder of God's everlasting promise that He will never leave or forsake His people, even in the midst of a conflict.

- Set a time for the meeting to begin and a time for the meeting to end. (People get tired and irritable after about one to two hours.) Exhaustion and irritability can cause even more conflict.
- Try to agree upon 1 to 3 outcomes for the meeting.
- Decide that there will be no violence, cursing, hitting, shouting or being disrespectful to anyone. (Don't be embarrassed to remind Christians that such behavior is possible but unacceptable). Discussing sensitive and moral issues can cause even dedicated Christians to "act-out." You want people to know that the meeting is a "safe" place to share their concerns, ideas and differences of opinions without being hassled or physically hurt.
- Stay with the subject. Discuss one item at a time. Don't push the group to resolve every issue in one meeting. Remember that some issues can't be resolved; they can only be managed.
- Only one person should speak at a time. A verbal "free-for-all" will do nothing but escalate the conflict.
- Be determined to find a solution that will benefit and satisfy both parties. Where there's a will, there's a way. Willing hearts, creative minds, and determined spirits can find miraculous solutions to problems.
- Watch, listen and learn, as other people share their convictions about things that matter in the church. You will learn where the "sensitive spots" are.
- Ask everyone involved in the conflict and participating in the meeting, "Are there any other ground rules that we need to put on the board before we begin our meeting? Can we all abide by these rules?" (Be firm. Stick to the rules).

> ***Conflicts occur, not because we are "hard of hearing," but because we are "hard of listening."***

2. Are you "speaking the truth in love" as the Apostle Paul advises?

- This is no time to be timid. The truth can't be dealt with by hiding it under the proverbial rug. Straight-forwardness and honesty have to be shared in a loving manner before conflict can be managed or resolved. The greater the number of people who speak up, the easier it is to determine the will of the majority.
- Remember you are not there to destroy, but to "build one another up." Hateful, harsh, critical, judgmental language can destroy relationships. The key is to eliminate problems—not people.

3. Take control of your own emotions.

- Be aware of your total communication. Albert Mehrabian states that we communicate 7% by our words, 38% by our tone and 55% by our body language. [1] So be aware of what your body is "saying." For example: pointing your finger in someone's face or in the face of a group and yelling, "I am not angry," communicates by your physical mannerisms that you are very angry and out of control.
- Take deep breaths to slow down your heart rate. Relax. Do not clench your fist as if you're going to fight, but put your hands in your lap. Do not stare or "glare." Do not grit your teeth or point your finger. Don't sound like a Marine Drill Sergeant, but talk in a slow, conversational tone. Be soft and gentle in volume and tone when you speak. Think about what you are saying and how your message is being understood.
- When you get scared or angry, your body gets into the "fight or flight" survival mode. When your hands are sweaty, your neck is red, your nostrils inflamed, your eyes dilated and

your heart pumping, it's so easy to want to "put people in their place," or even worse. So relax and remember, "The battle is the Lord's." You are dealing with His church, His work, and His people.

4. Listen before you speak.

- Listening is a skill that must be learned. Conflicts occur, not because we are "hard of hearing," but because we are "hard of listening." Try to understand the other person and "hear him or her out." You may change your opionion and how you feel about the issue/s at hand.

5. Take charge of the meeting. Facilitate with love, authority, and fairness.

- Have a marker-board, overhead projector, etc., to take notes. Be prepared. Many people are visual, having been conditioned by television, so writing down observations during a sharing session is valuable. Writing down a person's statement gives the person a chance to think before he/she continues to talk. It also often helps other persons get a new perspective on the conflict or problem at hand by seeing in writing what other people are thinking and feeling.

> ***Conflict can certainly be positive. Conflict can be a warning signal to a congregation that something rightfully so needs to be changed.***

6. Thank God for this conflict.

- Remember, anger and conflict, whether it is in your family or congregation, are warning signals that someone needs attention. Therefore, conflict can be very positive. Conflict can be a warning signal to a congregation that something needs to be changed in the way the church does or does not minister to others.

Honest dialogue can restore, reconcile, and transform a church into a more loving, ministering relationship.

An outsider looks in the church and sees - can you?

Members of Harmony Church where Mr. Watson, the Minister of Music, served were very discouraged. And during a recent community Thanksgiving meal, they began to gossip to members from a neighboring church. "You just can't talk to our Minster of Music," said one of the choir members.

"Yea, that's right," added another choir member, overhearing the conversation. "Every suggestion we make, he takes as criticism. He doesn't hear a word we say."

"And last Wednesday evening following choir practice, our organist 'let him have it.' She got right up in his face and told him she was not going to try to play a hymn that she had not rehearsed before the day of worship.

"Mr. Watson really got angry and told her, 'If you can't be sponta-neous, I'll find someone who can.'"

Some of the choir members were crying and stormed out of the church saying they were quitting the choir and maybe even leaving the church. One of the little ladies summed up the evening by saying, " I'm embarrassed to say there isn't much harmony in Harmony Church tonight.'"

Are you talking to each other in a way that can be understood?

New Pastor Milton Feldspar began to wonder what he'd gotton himself into.

Cartoon by John McPherson.[2]

HOW MANY OPTIONS HAVE YOU CONSIDERED?

8

"How many other options have you considered besides termination?"

It was a known fact that "good ol' boy" Billy Ray didn't like or even respect Mr. Frizzell, even though Frizzell was a disabled war veteran. Mr. Frizzell didn't necessarily care for Billy Ray or anyone else who disagreed with him, for that matter. It was the first of the month and time once again for Mt. Jewel Community Church's business conference, as the older folks traditionally called it.

The Sunday following the Fourth of July in this little Southern community proved to be hot, as usual. The sermon had been too long and people were hungry, but the conference began following morning worship as scheduled.

No, it wasn't the first time that Billy Ray had gone to sleep in church. And it certainly wasn't the first time that Mr. Frizzell had tried to "railroad" some personal project or decision through during a business conference. The discussion got hot and hotter over Mr. Frizzell's proposal. All of the shouting woke Billy Ray from a sound sleep. Billy Ray, only half-awake, could tell from the red faces and grumbling that he was missing something of major importance. Not wanting to be left out, he thought he would add his two-cent opinion. He stood up and pronounced, "I don't know what we're voting on, but if Mr. Frizzell is for it, I'm against it."

Some gasped in embarrassment, because visitors were present. Others giggled, and Mr. Frizzell stormed out of the church like an angry bull. Mr. Moderator, lost for words, took it upon himself to table the discussion and dismissed the business conference.

> ***It is apparent, that many congregations know more about "voting" than they do about resolving conflict.***

It is apparent that many congregations know more about "voting" than they do about resolving conflict. And if your church has a Billy Ray and a Mr. Frizzell, it's obvious that some people had rather fight and live in conflict than change.

Choosing sides and voting seems to be many congregations' favorite way of solving problems with staff, but in reality it's a good way to start a fight or perpetuate an old family feud in the church. Some congregations assume that the best approach is, "Put it to a vote."

Here are a few alternatives to firing your pastor or church staff that may prove to be helpful:

1. First, try spiritual discernment rather than polarizing the congregation with a vote.

Before the congregation decides to vote, the church body should pray for spiritual discernment concerning its conflict. Sometimes congregations wait too late to ask, "What is God's will in this matter?" Even though it has become a commercial slogan, ask yourself, WWJD—"What would Jesus do?" As you discern the spirits over this conflict, where is God leading?

2. Have you thought about calling in a church consultant?

When the level of conflict increases, it's easy to lose perspective. An outside church consultant can be an unbiased third party who will help with the issues at hand. Please note that it's always best if a church acts as a body to invite a third party. There are also professional mediators who can be hired for the sole purpose of helping each party to be heard and treated fairly in conflicted situations. The truth may be that the pastor really does need to leave. The consultant can help the body to make decisions that will redeem the pastor instead of destroying him.

Too often church members are embarrassed to call in experts. However, these same members don't mind calling an expert when one has a heart attack or breaks a leg. The body of Christ, likewise, should not hesitate to get help in a crisis.

3. Clarify your expectations of one another.

During the leading of listening skills workshops, Savage says that the failure to establish clearly agreed-upon expectations of one another can eventually lead to conflict. As a matter of fact, Savage often says in his workshops that we can't keep from being disappointed in one another at times. We are forever getting upset over things we feel people should do, but don't, and things people don't do that we feel they should do.

Clearly defined expectations of a pastor or staff person can greatly diminish the chances of conflict in a congregation.

One way to know what is expected of the pastor is to have a clearly written list of expectations discussed with church leadership and worked out with the pastor before he is elected. The congregation should also be acquainted with this written document. If the pastor does not know what is expected of him, he will fall short of someone's expectation. If the congregation does not know what the pastor expects of them, they too will fall short of his expectations.

Church members and pastor may expect too much from one another. Is your job description unrealistic? If so, rewrite it. Lower your expectations of your pastor or support the pastor in upgrading his pastoral and administrative skills. Have discussions with your pastor on what is most meaningful to the congregation. Reach agreements with which everyone can live.

4. What have you done to reconcile this conflict?

St. Paul says that Christians have been given the "ministry of reconciliation" (IICor.5:17-20). That means that Christians have a responsibility to do their part in bringing people to Christ. In a broader interpretation, Christians are also to be "peace makers," and bring people together. Church members are to be instruments of His grace and peace, and be role models showing the world how to deal with conflict.

5. Are you trying to take the easy way out?

Remember, firing the pastor may appear to be the easy way out.

6. Is your pastor or staff person "burned out?" If so, how can you minister to him or her and show grace?

Often ministers, church leaders, and other caregivers burn out, physically and emotionally. They continually go and give until they are exhausted. During burnout, caregivers sometimes see everyone as enemies. They become overly sensitive to criticism. They want to be left alone. When this happens, the pastor can easily cause conflict. Do you see any of these signs in your pastor? If so, they are a cry for help. Get your pastor some help so he can once again become "fired up," instead of just "fired."

An outsider looks in and sees – can you?

Rev. Travis looked exhausted. It was his first year as pastor following seminary. When he came to the church, he immediately was overwhelmed with administration, funerals, weddings, and several major crises. In addition, his wife of two years was pregnant with their first child. It seemed that between crises and committee meetings, he was never able to be home. It was obvious that something was wrong, because his sermons weren't polished, and he often appeared to be "day- dreaming"—even during counseling sessions. Several of the members felt the Pastor Search Committee had made a mistake in calling a minister fresh out of seminary.

Others loved the pastor and felt he could do no wrong. They often told him, "We think you are doing a fine job. Just ignore the criticism you are hearing."

But eventually, Rev. Travis was asked to resign because the mem-bers didn't know how to approach him about the disappointments and broken expectations that were becoming more frequently voiced throughout the church.

After Rev. Travis was fired, one of his supporters asked, "Did anyone ever suggest that our pastor see a doctor or counselor?"

With guilt settling upon the congregation, someone else asked, "I can't recall, but did we ever discuss other alternatives to firing our pastor?"

How many other alternatives have you considered besides termination?"

For all have sinned and fall short of the glory of God."

(Rom.3:23)

"If we say that we have no sin, we are deceiving ourselves, and the truth is not in us."

(IJn.1:8)

9

"Are you personally a part of the problem and in what way?"

I am reminded of a stately congregation in a Northern state by the name of Corinth Church. This old church was in a growing and changing community. The congregation had been in the process of searching for a combination staff person who could serve as minister of education and music. Staunch, proper and mild-mannered. Rev. Snow had supposedly been the pastor of this admired and respected congregation for nearly 20 years, but everyone knew Mrs. McEntire actually fulfilled the role of pastor. Whenever there was a major decision to be made, people would ask her opinion first. When a show of hands was asked for, everyone looked to see how Mrs. McEntire would vote. And then everyone else voted accordingly. Everyone assumed Mrs. McEntire's power and influence were the result of her forefathers' owning much of the county.

The search for the new staff person had been miraculously short, as if the proposed candidate had already been decided on before the Search Committee had even begun the process. Mrs. McEntire's nephew had recently graduated from one of the state's finest seminaries. Even though he had never worked with a staff and had only served a couple of small churches as part-time music director while in seminary, his Aunt McEntire just knew he was the "chosen one" for Corinth Church. When the reluctant candidate voiced concern over his lack of administrative skills, which would be a large part of his job description, Mrs. McEntire assured him he could do the job because she would be by his side to help him make decisions. This also concerned the prospective staff worker.

On the afternoon that the church was to hear the Search Committee's recommendation, Rev. Snow made a suggestion to Mrs. McEntire. (It was unusual for him to suggest anything to her). He suggested that the church needed to see a biographical sketch of the candidate and his proposed job description. Mrs. McEntire replied, "It is all taken care of. I have someone 'prompted' to make a motion and a second. And then I have a sister-in-law who will pass out a recommended financial package that I have prepared."

"Should the church not have the opportunity to ask questions and to discuss the whole process?" asked Rev. Snow.

"Yes, I suppose so," snipped Mrs. McEntire. "but I know what's best for our church, Reverend. I've been here much longer than you have. And the manner in which I propose to handle this situation will eliminate any embarrassing questions and possible hurt feelings. Several church members are related to my nephew, you know. And I've always firmly believed that the less a congregation knows and the fewer opportunities they have to question and debate matters, the smoother things go." Clutching her small white-zippered Bible, Mrs. McEntire raised her chin and piously added," And, Reverend, you know how the Lord despises conflict."

Numerous congregations have their own "Mrs. McEntires" to deal with, who either don't know or don't care that they are contributing to the mounting conflicts in the congregations where they are members. And congregations are also often unaware that they, too, are contributing to conflict under the facade of a joyful and unified congregation. This is so because the congregation refuses or doesn't have the skills or emotional and spiritual maturity to biblically confront their "Mrs. McEntires."

Conflict often arises when there is a misunderstanding or a misinterpretation of what is said or done, or in Mrs. McEntire's case, when appropriate and imperative information is withheld from the congregation. There is a tremendous amount of information that must flow continuously between numerous persons for congregations to function effectively and be healthy.

When conflict begins to surface in your congregation, here are a few questions to think about and some suggestions that may help you to slow down and resolve the conflict before it becomes an all-out war.

1. Have you prayed and sought out church members who have the gift of wisdom?

Don't gossip, but instead begin to work immediately for peace and unity with spiritually and emotionally mature Christians in your fellowship.

2. Have you gone to the pastor or other persons who may be causing the conflict?

Lovingly go in peace and tell them: "Brother or Sister, it appears to me you may be contributing to the conflict and disunity in our church. What is going on? How can we help?" (see Matthew 18:15-35).

3. What do you know of the facts?

Learn people's perception of the facts concerning the conflict you are facing. Go to the source of conflict—not to someone who merely gossips.

4. Have you immediately begun to address any concerns that could potentially become problems? "Nip it in the bud!"

Do not let the conflict or problem fester in the church. Any small "concern" may eventually cause much spiritual and emotional sickness if not dealt with.

5. Have you taken the pastor's side of the story—without asking any questions?

Just because church leaders are in places of power doesn't mean they are always right. Ministers are also fragile and fallible and at times unknowingly precipitate their own conflicts.

6. Have you periodically and "gently" asked your pastor these hard questions?

(a) Where do you think God is leading us? How do you hope to lead us and how do you plan to get us there? (Ask, because you may not want to go where he's leading.)

(b) Is this decision good for our congregation?

(c) Would you be open to meeting regularly with a support group for encouragement and mutual constructive feedback that could benefit you and our congregation?

7. Have you realized that you can't change people and that some people are difficult to deal with? You must be wise and have a plan in order to deal with them.

Keep your eyes and ears open to what is going on in the congregation. A healthy church is able to identify "concerns" and deal with them before they become problems. Paul reminds us that we are "flesh and spirit," and these war against each other, until we cannot do what we want to do, (Gal.5:16-17). I believe that people have a difficult time relating to one another, especially if they have had a horrible and painful background.

An outsider looks in and sees – can you?

Rev. Cash always moderated the business conference. Therefore he was not allowed (under *Robert's Rules of Order*) to make a motion. During a recent business meeting, he asked the Chairman of Deacons to moderate in his place as he stepped from behind the podium and made a motion that surprised the congregation.

"I believe having our traditional Homecoming, Mother's Day and Baby Dedication Day all on the same Sunday creates too many emphases for any one service," proclaimed the pastor. He continued: "The service is so full of activities that I'm usually left with about five minutes to preach a thirty-minute sermon. So, I make a motion to move our traditional Homecoming to the fall of the year, celebrate Mother's Day on the second Sunday of May, and do away with the Baby Dedication altogether. Mr. Moderator, I hope someone will second my motion."

There was a long silence in the congregation. Finally one young man said, "I second the motion."

"Is there any discussion?" asked the Chairman of Deacons. Church members squirmed in their seats and looked at one another, but no one said anything. "If there's not any discussion, I assume you are ready to vote," said the Chairman. "All in favor of this motion, let it be known by the uplifted hand." Hands slowly began to rise throughout the small congregation. In a somewhat subdued voice, the Chairman of Deacons responded: "And the vote carries in favor of the motion."

Relieved that a full service had been changed to a more manageable worship service, Rev. Cash smiled as he resumed his role as moderator for the rest of the business meeting. Little did he know that there was a volcano about to erupt in the congregation. He had not spoken to any church leaders about his decision to change a 150-year tradition in Shady Grove Church. And for 150 years no one at Shady Grove Church had challenged any decision that had been brought up during a Sunday morning business conference. But after the bell of Benediction chimed that day, there would be much talk, and decisions would be made that would affect Rev. Cash's ministry for the rest of his short stay as pastor.

Often congregations contribute to conflict by not saying anything, by not asking hard questions, and by not being bold enough to share their feelings and concerns about things that are precious to them—like a 150-year-old tradition.

Too often ministers make bold decisions without first talking with their congregation about how a decision might affect everyone else. Some ministers live by the motto, “It’s better to ask for forgiveness than to ask for permission.” They forget that no one is ever fired for asking permission.

Are you personally a part of the problem, and in what way?

10

"Do you have a written procedure for terminating church staff?

Be strong and courageous, do not be afraid or tremble at them, for the LORD your God is the one who goes with you. He will not fail you or forsake you."
(Deut: 31:6)

". . .let all things be done properly and in an orderly manner,"
(1Cor.14:40)

Reconciliation for conflicted situations is the emphasis of this book, but realistically, there are times when termination is warranted for the sake of the congregation's health and witness. Remember that sometimes love must be tough.

When termination seems to be the best course of action, check with your denominational leaders to see if written guidelines and procedures are available. Every denomination and local congregation is different, so for legal purposes a church should "do its homework" before considering termination. Documentation and appropriate Christ-like behavior are very important. You may want to talk with an attorney.

During the process of terminating a staff person, the congregation should be accurate, ethical, fair, gracious, and determined to do all it can to spare embarrassment and humiliation. This is not an opportunity to act with anger, bitterness or revenge.

Following are some suggestions you may consider if you believe termination is the best solution:

1. Termination should be a decision that is finally made by the whole church body.

A congregation should come to a spiritual consensus. Such a decision should be bathed in prayer and discussed by deacons, elders, trustees and/or other church leaders. The decision should not be made by a "parking-lot lynch mob." The Lord's business should be carried out in an open, honest, gracious, and biblical manner.

The congregation as a spiritual body would benefit by making decisions by consensus and should feel as led to terminate a minister as they did to call him. (In a consensus, a majority of members determine, without voting, that they feel led of God to make a particular decision.) Congregations come to a consensus in a variety of creative ways that may include prayer, discussion, worship and the contribution of various members. After all is said and done, the congregation "feels led of God" to make a decision. Those who differ feel heard and can usually agree to live with the decision. (See Chapter 5 for "Have you sought the will of God in this conflict?")

2. Consider "Planned Termination."

Another alternative to spontaneously firing the pastor is called "Planned Termination." Savage uses this term as he presents the "Role Renegotiation or Role Reconciliation Model" in his listening skills workshops. The model was first designed and used in the business arena by John J. Sherwood and John C.

Glidewell. Savage modified the model for church use. According to Savage, the model has become one of the most popular and helpful tools he uses with congregations. The model is used in teaching church members about the stages that all relationships go through and how relationships can be strengthened and made healthy. It is at the same time a historical and futuristic model showing how relationships either grow or "fall apart."

"Planned Termination" is a win/win concept. It provides for a pastor and a congregation to come to a clear understanding that they were not meant for each other and that both parties agree to go their separate ways instead of fighting and firing.

Picture this! Instead of the congregation firing its pastor or instead of the pastor abruptly leaving without explanation, the pastor would inform the congregation about his decision ahead of time or the congregation could take the lead in informing the pastor that it feels that the pastor and the congregation are mismatched. Either way, it takes a mature pastor and congregation to come to such an agreement.

For example, the pastor could say:

> Church family, as you know, my spiritual gift is evangelism. I love to introduce people to Jesus Christ as Savior. On the other hand, this congregation's passion is to feed the hungry, cloth the poor, and house the homeless. We are all God's ministers, but it is obvious that I do not have the gifts to match this congregation's ministries. Please give me time to seek the place of service that I can best use my gift of evangelism. I will leave within a reasonable amount of time (agreed upon by both of us) and allow you to call a minister with the gifts that will better match your needs and mission."

This is a win/win relationship even though the pastor and the congregation choose to discontinue their formal relationship.

3. Consider the democratic vote.

The plan of termination found in the "Policies and Procedures" manual of the Beaver Dam Baptist Church in Shelby, North Carolina, is an example of the democratic vote. All congregations would do well to write their own plan. Your denomination, regional minister, bishop or other denominational resources may offer guidelines in this procedure.

Sample Copy of
"Policies and Procedures for Termination of a Pastor
by Beaver Dam Baptist Church of Shelby, NC
(Used by permission)

A. Dismissal procedures may be initiated by the church in con-ference, the Fellowship of Deacons or the Personnel Committee.

(1) If the church in conference initiates dismissal and if there is dissension of the vote, the matter shall be referred to the Deacons who shall make investigation and in consultation with the Personnel Committee, shall make a recommendation to the church within two weeks after church action and two weeks before another vote is taken.

(2) If the Deacon Fellowship initiates the dismissal procedures, after consultation with the Personnel Committee, the deacons shall make a recommendation to the church two weeks before a vote is taken.

(3) If the Personnel committee initiates dismissal procedures it shall thoroughly explain its reasons to the Deacon Fellowship. The Personnel Committee shall make a recommendation to the church two weeks before a vote is taken.

B. The vote shall be by secret ballot.

Ballots shall be counted by a committee composed of Deacon Chairman, Deacon Secretary, Church Secretary, Head Usher, Trustee Chairman, and Church Clerk.

C. A majority of votes in favor of dismissal should be necessary for the pulpit to be declared vacant.

D. When the result of the voting is announced, the meeting shall adjourn without debate.

E. If the cause of dismissal is immoral or illegal conduct on the part of the pastor, termination should be immediate.

In all cases, except the above example, the church shall give the pastor thirty days' notice before termination. The church has the right to ask the pastor not to perform his pastoral duties during this thirty days. [1]

The above plan is *not very gracious* in giving thirty days to the pastor who has been terminated, but other churches feel that in today's economy a severance package equal to six months' pay is more satisfactory. Many churches would give two weeks; other churches would give the pastor only enough time to clean out his desk; still others might pack his belongings and mail them to him or set them on the street! A church should be very gracious in its severance package, considering the hardship to the pastor and his family when the pastor is terminated.

> ***Remember a church's goal should be to create a good working relationship with their pastor and staff so that termination will not***

Remember the words of St. Paul, "I THEREFORE, the prisoner of the Lord, entreat you to walk in a manner worthy of the calling with which you have been called, with all humility and gentleness, with patience, showing forbearance to one another in love, being diligent to preserve the unity of the Spirit in the bond of peace," (Eph.4:1-3).

11

Just for the Pastor: "It's never too soon to speak up!"

The late evangelist and popular pastors' conference speaker, Dr. Vance Havner, used to say, "It's too late to talk about draining the swamp when you're up to your neck in crocodiles." When should a pastor speak up when he detects conflict personally or within the congregation?

It has been said that churches have the biggest rug in town under which they sweep their problems. "Church secrets" can be detrimental to a congregation and pastor.

Congregations, like small towns, want to protect their image. They often believe, like individuals, that if they have problems, people will think they aren't committed to the Lord. A congregation is a family, and like any family it will have periods of conflict. But what do many congregations do? They keep silent! As the leader of the congregation, a pastor may also keep silent to help preserve unity in the congregation. If he would speak up even before the conflict is noticeable, he might help himself and the congregation to avoid conflict.

LaRue's survey of ministers across the country gives us insight into times when a pastor should "speak up." LaRue says:

> In retrospect, almost half of ousted pastors (those terminated or pressured to resign) think they could have done something to avoid being forced out. Resolving conflict was the primary action they wished they had taken sooner.

> ***"Church secrets" can be detrimental to a congregation and pastor.***

LaRue gives two suggestions for pastors seeking to resolve conflict: (1) "Resolve conflict as soon as possible; (2) Bring in an outside professional." Concerning using outside help, LaRue says, "Nearly 9 out of 10 churches using this method (outside professional) found it to be very helpful (49%) to somewhat helpful (38%) in easing tensions."

According to LaRue's survey, pastors who have been terminated or forced out "wished they had researched key topics more carefully when candidating."

Results of LaRue's survey note that:

45% wished they had explored former conflicts in the church.
43% wished that had explored the church's expectations of them.
30% wished they had discussed the Board's vision for the church.
25% wished they had explored their predecessor's reason for leaving.
18% wished they had known about the level of lay involvement.
11% wished they had explored the church's finances before they had taken this particular church as pastor.

> LaRue continues: "
> With a third of all churches having forced out the previous pastor and a tenth of all churches being repeat-offenders (having a history of three or more forced exits), pastors searching for a new church need to enter their next pastorate carefully.

In other words, pastors need to speak up before they go to a particular church as pastor or as a staff person.

The survey also reveals the following information about "forced-out" pastors:

82% wished they had talked to members of the congregation.
79% wished they had talked about Board Members.
68% wished they had talked with former pastors.
66% wished they had talked with their denominational leader.
4% wished they had spoken to other local pastors concerning conflict.

Therefore, it is obvious that pastors need to speak up, before they are called to a church, and they need to continue to speak up after they become pastors. LaRue encourages ministers to talk to the right people. He says:

> Knowing the right questions to ask, however, doesn't make a difference if you don't go to the people with the answers. Four out of five (82%) wish they had gone straight to the members of the congregation. About the same (79%) wish they had been more forthright with the members of the church board. [1]

Here are a few suggestions to aid pastors in speaking up before it's too late.

1. When you have a "gut sense" that something isn't right in the planning stages of a project or in the early stages of discussing some issue, speak up. Say to the individual or group, "I have some concerns I would like to voice, and I would like to see if others are having similar concerns."

2. It may not be appropriate to confront someone publicly, but if you are aware of inconsistencies, immorality, rudeness and abusive behavior that might be damaging to the congregation, then meet with the individual by appointment as soon as possible and voice your concerns and observations. If the person appears overly emotional, stressed-out or possibly harmful, be cautious and take someone with you to talk to this person. Remember: "Speak the truth in love." If you are wrong in your observations, apologize and move on. Better safe than sorry.

3. If there seems to be a lot of chattering about other topics and a lack of interest in discussing the topic at hand, say to the group, "It appears to me that we may be losing the focus of this meeting. Does anyone else sense that?" If so, help the meeting get back on track by exploring the commitment level in the group by asking each group member to share how they feel about the topic or issues that are being discussed in the present meeting.

4. If you are unhappy with what you hear during negotiations with a prospective church, speak up. Don't wait until you are called as a staff person and then begin to complain.

5. If you are criticized, agree only with that which is true concerning you; don't volunteer to be crucified for all the problems in the church. Say to the person or group, "You're right, I do need to improve in that area. Can you give me some suggestions?"

6. When you see lay persons or other church leaders pushing a personal agenda, say to the person or group, "Maybe we need to pray and gather more information before making a decision on this issue. Who would be willing to meet and pray before this

issue is brought to the church body?" This encourages everyone to discern the truth. The church's business meeting is not the place to say, "I see a potential problem here." But if you do not have prior knowledge, it's better to speak up then than after the decision is made.

7. If a fellow church member is being criticized or personally abused in a meeting or a parking lot session, say:

> I'm feeling very uncomfortable about what we're discussing. Since this person isn't here, we can't be certain that what we are sharing is 100% true. Our conversation may get back to this person, so let's be careful and fair in what we say. I'm sure we wouldn't want to damage a reputation. Let's try to be affirming and supportive of this church member.

(You are trying to be a role model and a peacemaker and teaching others indirectly how conflict often begins with unaccountable conversation and incorrect rumors.)

8. Pastor, when you feel uncomfortable, sense something is wrong, and/or feel led of God to say something, make your feelings known to the appropriate person, committee or church group. Remember what Havner said, "It's too late to talk about draining the swamp when you're already up to your neck in crocodiles."

9. Keep the congregation informed from the pulpit and by meetings, newsletters, and in general conversation about what you feel God's will is for the congregation. In order to keep the mission clearly focused, the pastor, staff and congregational leadership should periodically meet, (some recommend every 90 days) to keep the dream a live. And with all due respect, they may not be ready for your proposal. By getting feedback from the

congregation, you have a chance to talk with them and hear their concerns before a conflict begins over your proposal.

10. Constantly build relationships and create a climate of openness with your congregation and especially with your church leaders. If you teach people how to share openly, and you exhibit openness and non-judgmental sharing during the good times, your people will be more willing to hear you when conflict arises.

Tips on how to build relationships with your congregation that will help bring peace to your ministry and lessen conflict.

1. Love your people, laugh with them and enjoy being in their company. Spend time with your people, even those who cause you problems. It's the people, not the job!

2. Remember Jesus' teaching:
   "YOU SHALL LOVE THE LORD YOUR GOD WITH ALL YOUR HEART, AND WITH ALL YOUR SOUL, AND WITH ALL YOUR MIND." This is the great and foremost commandment. The second is like it, "YOU SHALL LOVE YOUR NEIGHBOR AS YOURSELF" (Mt.22:37-39).

   ". . . pray for those who persecute you." (Mt.5:44)

3. Remember the Apostle Paul's advice:
   ". . .encourage one another, and build up one another" (I Thess.5:11)
   ". . .Live in peace with one another" (I Thess.5:13)
   ". . .help the weak, be patient with all men" (I Thess.5:14)

"Do nothing from selfishness or empty conceit, but with humility of mind let each of you regard one another as more important than himself; do not merely lookout for your own personal interests, but also for the interests of others" (Phil.2:3-4).
"Never pay back evil for evil to anyone.... Never take your own revenge...Do not be overcome by evil, but overcome evil with good" (Rom.12: 17,19, 21).

4. Don't be distant from your people, cold, snobbish, rude or arrogant, but humble.

5. It's the minister's responsibility to teach the people about your responsibilities as pastor and person. Be open and honest. Don't live a secret life. Gently slip down from your pedestal and show them you are a human being with the feelings, desires, temptations and frustrations that they have. This will shock some people, so be gentle, patient and persistent in loving and teaching.

6. Admit you are wrong and have sinned when it happens. Ask for forgiveness and move on (I John 1:9).

7. *Very Important*: Model for your people how to be dissatisfied, upset and even very angry about an issue without "blowing up" and hurting other people and without pouting. Introduce them to the Christ who cleansed the temple and teach them about dealing with anger and conflict appropriately.

8. Learn to manage your anger. If you need counseling in this area, then get help now! Apologize when you lose your temper. Control your temper at home also. If you're angry at the church, don't abuse your family.

9. Don't ignore conflict. Work through the conflict and learn from it. A good question to ask after resolving conflict is, "What have we learned here and how will we handle this issue the next time?"

10. Learn your style of Conflict Management. Dr. Louis McBurney, a psychiatrist who has devoted his career to counseling ministers and missionaries in crisis, established the Marble Retreat in Marble, Colorado, where pastors, missionaries, church staff members, and other church professionals can seek new directions and new beginnings. He was interviewed in *Leadership Journal.* The article/interview was entitled "A Psychiatrist Looks At Troubled Pastors." McBurney says, "In trying to resolve conflict we usually take easy ways out." He mentions four ways that pastors often use—that don't work. McBurney is referring to the pastor and spouse, but these easy ways out are also used by pastors in relation to congregations.

One: Avoidance
McBurney says, "Running from it, pouting about it, and pretending it's not really happening seem initially more inviting than actually facing the conflict."

Two: Intimidation:
"If avoidance doesn't work, we try intimidation," says McBurney. "We threaten, cry, create power blocks, and quote Scripture."

Three: Manipulation:
"Sometimes we can't successfully intimidate, so we manipulate. This involves enticement, bribery, and withholding intimacy and personal influence."

Four: Deflection:
McBurney says, "Our final solution is usually deflection. Instead of focusing on the real issue, we deflect to issues that are safer, more urgent, and more comfortable." [2]

11. Work to find a win/win solution to your problems.

12. Assume your church family loves you and minister to them as if they do love you.

13. Join or begin a pastor's support group with healthy-minded pastors. In such an objective group you can test your ideas and role play how to deal with people with whom you find it difficult to communicate.

14. Invest in counseling from time to time. A confidential professional listener is worth the time and money.

15. Invest in Clinical Pastoral Education. This training is priceless and will challenge you to discover abilities and patterns of behaviors that can help you grow personally and professionally. (For information contact the Pastoral Care Department or the Chaplain's office at your local hospital)

16. Don't lose your sense of humor. Laugh at yourself and learn from your mistakes. You will be a healthier person and minister. Your people will love you for it.

"At the count of three, I want everyone to face the person next to hir and get rid of your hostilities and be happy human beings."

ırtoon by Joseph Farris, Leadership, Spring Quarter, 1980, Vol.1, No.2, 21. Used by permissic

CONCLUSION

In 1987, my wife Pam and I and our two-year-old son Nathan, went as foreign missionary volunteers to Zimbabwe, Africa, for 30 days. We spent most of our time at the Sanyati Baptist Hospital, where Pam had served as a Nurse Midwife.

Before leaving America, we bought a carrier for Nathan that strapped on my back like a backpack. This left my hands free to carry luggage. Nathan loved it.

Once, following a long day of preaching and visiting, I decided to take a leisurely walk through the village. Since Nathan was too small for a long walk, I carried him in my backpack, his hands often holding onto my shoulders. As I walked by the Sanyati hospital where Pam was volunteering that evening, I passed a young African boy sweeping the sidewalks. He stopped sweeping and stared at me. African women carry babies on their backs, but African men do not. The young boy yelled to me, "Can he feel your love?" I thought that was a peculiar question. Again he yelled loudly, "Can he feel your love?" That's a question every parent should ask his or her children. It's the question that every married person should ask his or her spouse. And it's the question every pastor should ask his congregation, "Can you feel my love?" It's the question church members should ask their pastor, "Can you feel my love?"

The Bible says the greatest virtue is love. Is love the key to handling conflict? If members compassionately loved one another enough to give each other mercy and forgiveness, would not a lot of conflict be "nipped-in-the-bud?"

Francis Frangipane, in his book, *Holiness, Truth and the Presence Of God* says,

> Most of us are afraid to live in the exposed, vulnerable state of the art that love demands. As Christians, we talk about love much more often than we live it. But real love is daring, it is exciting. It boldly conquers evil, then heals and reunites with God those that it loves. It is aggressive. . . . God's love is not just forgiving, it is for living. As we overcome bitterness and climb out of the pit of unforgiveness—suddenly, we are as bold as a lion. Love grows from being a commandment to becoming an adventure! [1]

Christians love to preach about love. It is supposedly the cornerstone on which the church is built. But it's evident that many had rather talk about love than put it into practice. When the first evidence of conflict occurs in a congregation, there is a challenge to relate to people in love. As Frangipane indicates, love is aggressive. Love reaches out and takes control of the situation. Love confronts. Love challenges. Love explains. Love demands to be heard. Love forgives and lives and lets others live. Love is as bold as the African sky, and love longs to captivate our hearts.

Do we love God enough to honestly put love into practice? Jesus says:

> 'YOU SHALL LOVE THE LORD YOUR GOD WITH ALL YOUR HEART, AND WITH ALL YOUR SOUL, AND WITH ALL YOUR MIND.' This is the great and foremost commandment. The second is like it, 'YOU SHALL LOVE YOUR NEIGHBOR AS YOURSELF.' On these two commandments depend the whole Law and the Prophets (Mt.22:37-40).

If we really love God; we must *show* that love. And this expression of love should be evident among God's people.

A congregation may spend the majority of the time ministering or fighting. Savage reminds us that we only have so much time and energy. The average congregation should be spending 80% of its time in ministry and only 20% of its time in maintenance (administration and handling conflict, etc). Remember that conflict is inevitable, but what happens in a lot of congregations is that the percentage is lived out in reverse. Members spend 80% of their time dealing with conflict, leaving only 20% of their time and energy for ministry. What a shame and poor testimony! Either we choose to allow our compassion for Christ to consume us or controversy and conflict will consume us.

Gordon MacDonald, author and former pastor of Grace Chapel in Lexington, Massachusetts, was interviewed in *Leadership Journal* with four other ministers. The result of their interview was an article, "Conflict: Facing it in yourself and in your church." MacDonald challenges us not to lose the reality of who the church is, therefore helping us to put conflict into perspective. He says:

> We should never underestimate the complexity of the church. It's the only institution that takes care of people from the cradle to the grave. Part of the reason there is conflict in the church is that it deals with spiritual problems. People expect the church to be a healing, loving experience, but they often find conflict. They may also find anger, jealousy, and lust. At the church, we need to come together and confront our own sinfulness, and the sinfulness of one another. Thus we ought not be surprised when someone opens a door and "real life" springs out. That's what the church is all about—to deal with real life redemptively. [2]

"The Body of Christ" will face conflict. And as MacDonald says, "Don't be surprised when people, even Christians, act like human beings." It is my prayer that church members will take the suggestions and the tools in "*Pastor, We Need To Talk!*" and relate to other members and their pastors in love and forgiveness. That is living redemptively.

It is rarely appropriate to terminate a pastor or church staff person. May an unselfish, caring, loving, redemptive spirit always be the first choice.

AFTERWORD

John S. Savage, D.Min.
John Savage Resources, LLC
Reynoldsburg, Ohio

After Lucy, of the "Peanuts" comic strip, finishes a lecture that she has just given to Charlie Brown, Charlie says, "Now that I know that, what do I do?"

That is basically the question to ask after reading any book, let alone this good work by Dennis Hester.

Because this book is filled with an amazing array of resources and information, the following may be helpful to bring this book into your reality.

For your personal reflection:

1. Name the most significant learning, idea, or concept. An example: It is crucial to open up communication between persons during the time of conflict.
2. What set of emotions does this book evoke in you? Where does it push you up against your own walls and make you take a look at yourself, not just the behaviors of others?
3. How does it help you understand how you may take part in the conflicts in your own church?
4. How do you manage your own personal conflicts? To the degree that you are internally conflicted, to that degree you

are often externally conflicted. What goes on in you is more important than what goes on around you. If you cannot manage your own inner conflict, it is not difficult to see how you would run from external conflict. This book is devoted to extroperceptive (outside yourself) concepts. Turn those concepts inward and ask how you are like your conflicted church. If your church avoids conflict, how do you avoid conflict? Or what is there in you that you want to avoid that will keep you from engaging the conflict in your congregation?

For Group Reflection:

1. This book would make an excellent resource for a ten-week Sunday School class. Read one chapter a week. Discuss its implication for your current church situation.
2. At the end of Dennis Hester's book is a wonderful list of Scriptures (Appendix D). Have each person in the group read a series of Scriptures and discuss them in a prayer group or Sunday School class.
3. After reading this book, have individuals in the group write a brief history of their own experience in managing conflict. Have them reflect on the family that raised them and how that family demonstrated the resolution of conflict or the lack thereof.
4. Distribute between individuals in a group the task of creating a book table of as many printed resources as you can find about conflict in business and in the church. There are many such resources. Just type "Conflict" in one of the search engines on the Internet, i.e. Yahoo or Google, and see the hundreds of books that will come up for your consideration.
5. This book should stimulate your interest in the field of conflict management. Set up a one- to three-year training sequence to teach people how to manage conflict including

starting with children in your Sunday School. There are many, many such resources available. It would be a wonderful gift to your people, because these skills can be used all your life. Your work, home, friends, and church will be enhanced just because you read this book.

6. Take some of the key ideas from this book, i.e. the different levels of conflict from Speed Leas, and put them on large posters and place them around your church. Print out some of the key Scriptures that Dennis has quoted and place them before the people.
7. Finally: Do not put this book on a bookshelf, but keep it on your desk to review over and over again. You will soon discover that ideas from it will keep cropping up in your thoughts, behaviors and the way you treat others. Make it a gift to yourself. Remember that every person is radically gifted and radically flawed. Be sure to say thanks for the gifts and to forgive the flaws.

Appendix A

Study Questions for Church Leaders and Congregations

This book, along with the following questions, can be used during church staff meetings for the discussion and training of deacons, elders, and other church leaders and for laypersons alike. This study can be conducted "chapter by chapter" or by priority—"what the congregation feels is their greatest need at present." The study can be conducted during a Bible study, Discipleship Training, retreats, and seminars or in the classroom. The time allowed for this study depends upon the needs of individual congregations. The study questions can be used during a one-hour Bible study, an ongoing Discipleship Training study that lasts for several weeks, a one-day workshop or a three-day retreat. The key is to be open and honest during the study and create a safe and caring place where people feel free to share concerns and ideas that will help the congregation or parties to learn how to deal with conflict.

Remember that this is a time of learning and sharing. You will be trying to get insights into your church's history with church staff, as well as exploring how your church deals with conflict.

As you begin, pray that God will give you wisdom and direction. Give your group time to read the chapter that will be discussed.

Chapter 1, "At what level or stage of conflict is your congregation?"

1. After examining Speed B. Leas' five levels of conflict, at what level or levels of conflict would you say your congregation is?
2. Do you have a conflict that everyone can identify and is willing to try to resolve without the desire to win or hurt others? At what level of conflict are these objectives stated?

3. At what level does conflict in the congregation become unmanageable?
4. At what level of conflict is a congregation beginning to experience serious trouble that requires the help of a third-party?
5. At what level of conflict does the congregation begin to mix personalities with issues so that the problem or conflict can no longer be clearly defined?
6. Name the level of conflict whereby conflicted parties shift from wanting to win to wanting to get rid of person/s?
7. Has your conflict been so painful that all your primary thoughts are about revenge and "getting back" at those who have hurt you? How does this relate to Rom.12: 14-21?
8. What stage describes the church as cold, indifferent and non-responsive; and what is recommended before the church can move from this level to experience healing?

Chapter 2, "Do you know the sources of your conflict?"

1. After carefully examining Pneuman's nine common sources of conflict in churches, choose the sources of conflict that are causing your church the most difficulty. (See Appendix E, for Pneuman's Checklist for Conflicted Congregations.) Ask each member in your group to identify the sources of conflict he/she chose. Observe if members chose the same sources of conflict.
2. How did this conflict or these conflicts begin?
3. How did your parents or other significant persons you know handle conflict?
4. How do you personally handle conflict and how might that behavior contribute to your church's present conflict?
5. How has your congregation handled conflict and has it been an effective and healthy method?

6. After you have read this chapter, what plan of action seems best to resolve your present conflict or conflicts?
7. What were some of the reasons for conflict in the book of Acts and how were those conflicts handled?

Chapter 3, "How are you working for unity?"

1. How are you (pastor and/or congregation) working to create unity in your congregation?
2. Are you denying or ignoring that there are problems in your church (no matter how small) that need to be addressed?
3. According to Eph.4: 1-3 a congregation must diligently work to preserve unity in the church family. What are you doing to stay unified as a congregation?
4. Review the seven questions under "Consider these questions that work for unity," and discuss them in your group.
5. Steven Covey encourages people to try to understand other people first instead of trying to get them to understand your perspective first. If there is presently a conflict in your congregation do you fully understand the reason/s for the conflict and how the other party feels about this issue?
6. What is happening in the story at the end of the chapter with Rev. Williams and his congregation?

Chapter 4, "Are you trying to solve a problem or get rid of a person?"

1. As the title of this chapter asks, "Are you honestly trying to solve a problem or get rid of a person?" What evidence do you have for your choice?
2. Does your congregation affirm and encourage everyone, especially the church staff? If so how does this happen? If not, what can you do to be better encouragers according to I Thess.5: 11, 14?

3. Has your congregation ever tried to eliminate or fire a staff person? Looking back, how could this process have been better dealt with?
4. If you have ever fired a minister or staff person or "pressured" an employee to leave, did you notice any of the problems listed in Chapter 4 taking place? Was it worth firing that person? How could that whole issue have been dealt with differently?
5. Discuss some or all of the eight questions at the end of Chapter 4.
6. In the story at the end of Chapter 4, who was the "group in the parking lot," and how much power did they have? What other approach could the congregation have taken in dealing with Pastor Jones' tardiness?

Chapter 5, "Have you sought the will of God in this conflict?"

1. As you deal with conflict are you remembering the "mind of Christ," according to Phil.2: 3-5? How is this attitude revealed or not revealed?
2. How is God at work in your congregation even in the midst of conflict?
3. In this chapter you are encouraged to remember four principles during conflict. Discuss these principles and how the congregation can benefit from them.
4. How can your congregation put into practice the five suggestions in seeking the will of God in the midst of conflict?
5. Examining the story about Rev. Haggard at the end of this chapter, how would your congregation go about sharing with your pastor that the congregation can also have a word from God concerning God's will for the church? How does the congregation and the pastor bring together both of their visions/desires for the future of the congregation?

Chapter 6, "Are you treating every person as Christ would?"

1. Does your pastor and congregation preach, teach and express forgiveness easily? If not, why not? How could forgiveness be better expressed in your worship and lifestyle as a Christian congregation?
2. During worship and Bible study in your congregation, do you feel "beaten down," or "lifted up?" Which is preached and taught more in your congregation: forgiveness or judgment? How does this make you feel?
3. In John 2: 13-25 Jesus cleared the temple with a whip and overturned the money changers' tables. Discuss this text in light of the popular belief that Christians are not supposed to get angry.
4. John Savage says, "Anger is nothing more than a heightened 'cry for help.'" If there are persons who are expressing anger or engaged in inappropriate behavior in your congregation, what may be the message or messages they are trying to get you to hear? What is driving their anger?
5. After thinking about the four common ways people handle anger, how does each of you in this group handle anger during conflict?
6. How can your congregation put into practice the guidelines that God's Word gives in how to handle conflict?
7. How can the congregation help Rev. Jackson and Deacon Lewis resolve their differences?

Chapter 7, "Are you talking to each other in a way that can be understood?"

1. Do you have a plan to handle conflict?
2. Conduct a role-play to handle a conflict in your congregation, using the suggestions from Chapter 7. Which suggestions do you need to work on most?

3. What have you learned or not learned from former conflicts in your congregation?
4. There is obviously a conflict among choir members and Rev. Watson, the Minster of Music. How can this conflict be turned into a win/win situation instead of a war? Divide the group. One side role-plays a Minister of Music. The other side role-plays choir members. Take turns and justify why you are upset, angry and ready to quit. Now switch sides. Tell the group how you feel and why you are angry.
5. What could be done to put the harmony back in Harmony Church?

Chapter 8, "How many other options have you considered besides termination?"

1. Discuss an incident in which you dismissed a staff member. Can you remember if any other options were discussed? If yes, what were they and why were they not workable suggestions?
2. Does voting on matters create harmony or conflict in our church?
3. How do you understand spiritual discernment and consensus? Is spiritual discernment and working toward a consensus something your church would be open to learning and putting into practice?
4. Out of the six options to firing that are listed, which one/s would be most helpful to your congregation at this time or in the future?
5. Does your pastor show signs of "burnout" and, if so, what can you do to help him?
6. In the story at the end of this chapter how could the church have ministered to Rev. Travis instead of firing him? How can broken expectations be renegotiated?

Chapter 9, "Are you personally a part of the problem and in what way?"

1. Considering the conflict you are presently in or as you think about a past conflict, how did you contribute to the conflict?
2. On a scale of 1 to 10, how much of a sinner do you see yourself in light of Rom.3: 23, and 1Jn.1: 8?
3. In this chapter the author lists seven suggestions that may help a group to pause and resolve conflict before it becomes an all-out war. How can you put these suggestions into practice immediately?
4. Describe what a healthy church should look and act like. In light of what you have learned in this study, how does a healthy congregation handle conflict?
5. How does Rev. Cash get himself into trouble and cause a conflict in 150-year old Shady Grove Church? Did Rev. Cash have a valid reason for wanting to change the tradition of the church? If you had been a member of Shady Grove Church on the morning of the vote, what would you have said or done? Why do you think no one objected during discussion? Has your church ever experienced conflict because you kept silent? Why did you keep silent? How can you change this trend in yourself and your church?
6. Does your church staff or church members live by the motto: "It's better to ask for forgiveness than to ask for permission?" What is the problem with this motto?

Chapter 10, "Do you have a written procedure for terminating church staff?"

1. Do you have a written procedure for terminating church staff? If so, is it a good, well-written procedure?
2. If you don't have such a procedure, do you see a need to create such a policy? Why should this document be considered? If not, why?

3. In light of past firings in your church, would such a document have helped the congregation in knowing how and why to terminate that person?
4. How do you feel about even discussing such a policy and document?
5. Do you prayerfully believe that termination is presently your best option in dealing with your pastor or staff member? If so, why?
6. What do we think about "Planned Termination?" Is this a viable option for you?
7. How do we feel about "voting someone out" of your church?
8. Discuss "Policies and Procedures" for termination of a pastor by Beaver Dam Baptist Church of Shelby, NC. Using this document as a starting place, discuss what you like or don't like about this document. What changes do you need to make before your church could adopt this document as "your" policy and procedure when having to terminate a pastor or staff person?
9. What have you learned from this study?
10. What changes will you make after having shared in this study?
11. What is a "fair" severance package for a staff person and his or her family, following termination?"

Study Questions Worksheet

Study Questions Worksheet

Appendix B

End Notes

Introduction:

1. Mike Huckabee, "When You Want to Fire Your Minister" *The Deacon*, Oct/Nov/Dec, 1992, 18.

2. Research Projects on *"Forced Termination and Church Conflict,"* From 1984 - 1998, Compiled by Norris E. Smith, LifeWay Christian Resources of the Southern Baptist Convention, Nashville, TN.

3. Told by church consultant Edward B. Bratcher, author of, *The Walk-On-Water Syndrome, "Dealing with Professional Hazards in the ministry,"* (Waco,Texas: Word Books Publishers, 1984).

4. Cartoon used by permission from Cartoonist Jonny Hawkins. 10/9/00. A similar cartoon first used in *Leadership*. Winter, Vol.19, No.1, 1998, 36.

Chapter 1

1. Speed B. Leas, *Moving Your Church Through Conflict,* Bethesda, Maryland: Alban Institute, Inc., 1985, 19-22.

2. "Problem Solving/Decision Making Process," created by Rod L. Reinecke and Ruth R. Wright, ConTrOD ASSOCIATES, Burlington, NC.

Chapter 2

1. Roy Pneuman, "Nine Common Sources of Conflict in Churches," *Action Information*, Alban Institute, March/April, Vol.18, No.2, 1992, 1-5.

2. Arlin J. Rothauge, *Sizing Up A Congregation,* The Domestic and Foreign Missionary Society, 1995, Revised Edition May, 1996, 5-36.

3. Roy M. Oswald, *Making Your Church More Inviting,* Bethesda, Maryland: Alban Institute, Inc., 1992, 5-17.

4. Harris W. Lee, *Effective Church Leadership,"A Practical Sourcebook,"*
(Minneapolis: Augsburg, 1989), 39-42.

Chapter 3

1. Stephen R. Covey, Habit 5, "Seek First to Understand, Then to Be Understood," *The 7 Habits of Highly Effective People* (New York: A Fireside Book, Simon & Schuster, 1989), 237.

2. John Savage, *Listening & Caring Skills, "A Guide for Groups and Leaders"* (Nashville: Abingdon Press, 1996), 10.

   Ideas and statements that reference Dr. John Savage, other then the above quote from his book, *Listening & Caring Skills,* were taken from his Listening Skills, Leadership and Conflict Management workshops, lead by Dr. Savage, and attended by the author.

Chapter 4

1. John LaRue, "Special Report, Forced Exits: Personal Effects," *Your Church,* November/December, 1996, 64.

2. John LaRue, "Special Report, Forced Exits: High-Risk Churches," *Your Church,* May/June, 1996, 72.
3. George Barna, *Today's Pastors,* (California: Regal Books, 1993), 154.

4. Robert D. Dale, *Pastoral Leadership*, (Nashville: Abingdon Press, 1986), 91.

Chapter 7

1. Albert Mehrabian, "Communication Without Words," *Psychology Today*, Vol.2 No.4, September, 1968, 53-55.
2. Cartoon used by permission from cartoonist John McPhearson.

Chapter 10

1. "Policies and Procedures for Termination of a Pastor," Beaver Dam Baptist Church, 123 Beaver Dam Baptist Church Road; Shelby, NC 28152.

Chapter 11

1. John LaRue, "Special Report, Forced Exits: How to Avoid One," *Your Church*, January/February, 1997, 88.

2. Louis McBurney, "A Psychiatrist Looks at Troubled Pastors," *Leadership*, Spring, Vol.1, No.2, 1980, 117.

3. Joseph Farris, *Leadership*, Spring 1980, Vol.1, No.2. 21.

Conclusion

1. Francis Frangipane, *Holiness Truth and the Presence of God*, (Cedar Rapids: Arrow Publications, 1986), 103-104.

2. Gordon MacDonald, Conflict: "Facing It in Yourself and in Your," *Leadership*, Spring 1980, Vol.1 No.2, 36

Appendix C

Resources and Contact Information

One only has to go to a local bookstore, library, or the Internet and click on "communication, mediation or conflict management and conflict resolution" to find an awesome amount of resource material on these topics.

The following resources provide training in communication, conflict management and conflict resolution skills and a host of other leadership and managerial training for ministers and churches. Many of these sources also provide counseling, consulting and various other support related to congregations, ministers, businesses and non-profit organizations.

Start with your local, state, and national denominational offices, mediation centers, church related ministries and organizations that offer counseling, consulting, leadership training and support for church leaders, congregations and non-profit organizations.

Selected Reading

1. Alessandra, Tony and Paul Hunsaker. *Communicating at Work.* New York: A Fireside Book/Simon & Schuster, 1993.

2. Anderson, Leith. *Dying For Change: An Arresting Look At New Realities Confronting Churches and Para-Church Ministries.* Minneapolis, MN: Bethany House Publishers, 1990.

3. Bagby, Daniel G. *Understanding Anger in the Church.* Nashville: Broadman Press, 1979.

4. Barna, George. *User Friendly Churches*. Ventura: CA: Regal Books/Gospel Light, 1991.

5. Barna, George. *The Frog in the Kettle*. Ventura: CA: Regal Books/Gospel Light, 1990.

6. Barna, George. *The Power of Vision*. Ventura: CA: Regal Books/ Gospel Light, 1992.

7. Barna, George. *Turn Around Churches: How to Overcome Barriers to Growth and Bring New Life to an Established Church*. Ventura: CA: Regal Books/Gospel Light, 1993.

8. Brinkman, Rick and Rick Kirschner. *Dealing With People You Can't Stand. How to Bring Out the Best in People at Their Worst*. McGraw-Hill, Inc., 1994.

9. Cullinan, Alice R. *Time For A Checkup*. Fort Washington Pennsylvania: Christian Literature Crusade, 1994.

10. Dale, Robert D. *Leadership for a Changing Church*. Nashville: Abingdon, 1998.

11. Dale, Robert D. *Leading Edge.* Nashville: Abingdon, 1996.

12. Gangel, Kenneth O. and Samuel L. Canine. *Communication and Conflict Management in Churches and Christian Organizations*. Nashville: Broadman Press, 1992.

13. Halverstadt, Hugh F. *Managing Church Conflict.* Louisville, KY: Westminister/John Knox Press.

14. Hendricks, William D. *Exit Interviews: Revealing Stories of Why People are Leaving the Church.* Chicago: Moody Press, 1993.

15. Lavender, Lucille. *They Cry Too! Pastors Don't Belong on Pedestals.* Grand Rapids, Michigan: Pyranee Books/ Zondervan Publishing House, 1976.

16. Leas, Speed B. *A Lay Person's Guide to Conflict Management.* Bethesda, Maryland: Alban Institute, Inc., 1979.

17. Leas, Speed B. and Kittlaus, Paul. *Church Fights: Managing Conflict in the Local Church.* Philadelphia: The Westminster Press, 1973

18. Morris, Danny E. and Charles M. Olsen. *Discerning God's Will Together: A Spiritual Practice for the Church.* Bethesda, Maryland: The Alban Institute, Inc., 1997.

19. Olsen, Charles M. *Transforming Church Boards, into Communities of Spiritual Leaders.* Bethesda, Maryland: Alban Institute, Inc., 1995.

20. Oswald, Roy M. and Speed B. Leas. *The Inviting Church: A Study of New Member Assimilation.* Bethesda, Maryland: Alban Institute, Inc., 1987.

21. Perry, Robert L. *Pass the Power Please.* Richmond, VA.: Organizational Health Association, Inc., 1995

22. Satir, Virginia. *Making Contact.* Berkeley, CA: Celestial Arts, 1976.

23. Saussy, Carroll. *The Gift of Anger: A Call to Faithful Action.* Louisville, KY: Westminister, John Knox Press, 1995.

24. Schaller, Lyle E. *Strategies for Change.* Nashville: Abingdon Press, 1993.

25. Stoop, David and Stephen Arterborn. *The Angry Man: "Why does he act that way?"* Dallas: Word Publishing, 1991.

26. Weese, Carolyn. *Eagles in Tall Steeples: Insights into Pastors and the People They Pastor.* Nashville: Oliver Nelson/Thomas Nelson Publishers, 1991.

27. Weisinger, Hendric. *Anger At Work: Learning the Art of Anger Management on the job.* New York: William Morrow and Company, 1995.

Consultants/Mediators, Trainers and Advocates for Congregations

1. Dr. John S. Savage, D.Min.
   John Savae Resources LLC E-mail: jsavage2@insight.rr.com

2. Lombard Mennonite Peace Center Office: (630)627-0507
   101 W. 22nd St., Suite 206 E-mail: Admin@LMPeaceCenter.org
   Lombard, IL 60148-4527 Website: www.LMPeaceCenter.org

   The LMPC equips persons with skills to resolve conflict in the family, church, school, workplace and community using biblical principles.

3. Bill Easum. Email: Easum@aol.com
   Senior Partner, The Effective Church Group www.effectivechurch.com

4. Barna Research Group, Ltd.
   www.Barna.org

   The nation's largest full-service marketing research company dedicated to the needs of the Christian community. Their goal is to serve Christ by keeping the Church well-informed about the society in which we have been called to minister. Barna is the best-selling author of such books as: *The Frog in the Kettle, User Friendly Churches, What Americans Believe, The Power of Vision, Turn Around Churches and Today's Pastors*.

7. The Alban Institute
   Alban at Duke Divinity School
   www. Alban.org

   Alban books are now published by Rowman & Littlefield
   www.rowman.com/page/albanbooks

Appendix D

Selected Scripture Cross-Referenced by Topic

Anger
Genesis 4:1-8 •25-27
Psalm 37:8 85
Proverbs 14:16-17 14:29 15:1 16:32 21:14 25:23
Jonah 4:9
Matthew 5:21-26
Mark 3:5 10:13-14
John 2:13-17 11:21
Ephesians 4:25-32
Colossians 3:5-17, 9-20

Comfort
Isaiah 49:13 57:18 61:1-3
II Corinthians 1:3-7 2:5-11

Conflict
Numbers 20:2-13
I Samuel 18-31
Proverbs 26:17
Matthew 12:36-37, 16:23
Luke 2:34-35, 10:25-37 10:38-42
Acts 15:1-35, 15:36-41 17:1-9, 28:22-27
Romans 12:9-21
I Corinthians 3:1-3, 3:4-9
Galatians 2:11-21, 5:16-17
Ephesians 4:25-32
Philippians 4:1-3
II Timothy 2:16, 2:23-26

Encouragement
I Corinthians 3:16-17
Galatians 4:7, 5:22-26
Ephesians 1:3-6, 1:13-14 6:10-17
Colossians 3:5-17
I Thessalonians 5:1-15

Forgiveness
Psalm 32:1-2, 51, 130
Proverbs 19:11
Isaiah 1:18
Matthew 6:14, 18:21-35
Mark 11:25
Luke 17:1-4
John 8:10-11
II Corinthians 13:11-13
Ephesians 4:25-32
Colossians 3:5-17
I John 1:8-9

Healing
Psalm 51, 147:3

Isaiah 6:9-10, 57:18

Hope
Psalm 34:17-19, 42:11
43:5, 71:5, 85
119:71, 130
John 10:10
Romans 12:9-21

Listening
Isaiah 6:9-10
Jeremiah 29:12
Acts 28:28
Matthew 17:5, 18:15-17
Luke 10:38-42
Acts 15:13, 28:28
James 3:1-12

Love
Leviticus 19:18
Proverbs 10:12
Jeremiah 31:3
Matthew 5:43-48
22:34-40
Luke 10:25-37
15:11-32
John 3:16, 13:34-35
15:12-17, 16:26-28
I Corinthians 13:4-8,13
II Corinthians 1:3-7, 2:5-11
Galatians 3:28-29
Ephesians 2:1-22, 4:1-6
4:15-16
Philippians 2:1-4
Colossians 3:5-17
I Thessalonians 5:11-22
I John 2:9-11, 3:14,20
4:7-8, 4:10,21
5:1-3, 5:11-22
II Thessalonians 2:16-17
I Peter 1:3,13,21

Mercy
I Chronicles 21:13
Psalm 28:6, 40:11
69:16, 143:1
Proverbs 28:13
Isaiah 55:7, 63:9
Jonah 4:2
Micah 6:8, 7:18
Hosea 6:6
Zechariah 7:9
Matthew 5:7
Luke 1:50, 6:36
Romans 9:15-16, 12:1,8
Ephesians 2:4-5
Titus 3:3-5
Hebrews 4:16
James 2:13, 3:17
Jude 1:2

Peace
Psalm 29:11, 34:14
Proverbs 13:3, 26:22
Matthew 5:38-48, 6:33-34
John 14:27, 15:27

I Corinthians 1:9-10
Ephesians 4:1-6
II Thessalonians 3:16

Peacemakers
Matthew 5:7-9
Romans 12:9-21
Ephesians 2:14
I Peter 3:8-12

Restoration
Psalm 77, 85, 130, 147:3
Proverbs 25:21-22
Isaiah 1:18, 2:4, 57:18, 61:1-3
Jeremiah 30:17
Matthew 18:15-20
Mark 10:43-44
Luke 15:11-32, 17:1-4
John 8:10-11, 13:15
Romans 12:3-21
Ephesians 2:11-22

Security
Psalm 55:22
Isaiah 43:1-3
John 10:27-30, 14:18
Jude 1:24

Unity
Psalm 133:1
John 17:20-23
I Corinthians 1:9-10, 10:16-17, 12:12-26, 13:4-8,13, 14:40
II Corinthians 2:5-11, 5:18-21
Galatians 3:28-29, 5:22-26
Ephesians 2:1-22, 4:1-6, 4:15-16, 4:25-32, 5:15-21
Philippians 1:3, 1:27-28, 2:1-4 3:14-16, 4:1-3
Colossians 3:5-17
I Thessalonians 5:11-22
I Peter 3:8-12

Appendix E

The Source Checklist for Conflicted Congregations By Roy W. Pneuman and Margaret E. Bruehl PB Associates

Congregational Elements	Conditions	Specifics About This Congregation
PURPOSE * Values/beliefs re: the Church	Differences over	
* Vision, purpose, mission, direction, identity	Absent, ambiguous or disagreement about	
* Programs and budget	Not reflective of mission	
* Strategic Plan: Goals/Objectives	Lacks action/ accountability	
STRUCTURE * Roles and responsibilities (especially of the pastor (s))	Absent, ambiguous or disagreement about	
* Procedures, policies and standards	Absent, ambiguous or disagreement about	
* Organization, functioning and style of relating	Does not fit with current size of the congregation	
RESOURCES * People, talent, time, finances, facilities, ideas, etc.	Scarcity or overabundance	

RELATIONSHIPS * Ways of dealing with differences	Absent or dysfunctional	
* Communication practices and sharing of information	Ambiguous, inaccurate or insufficient	
* Cultural Styles: Regional, ethnic, racial, gender, age, education, etc.	Differences over	
* Response to changing environment beyond church property	Differences over	
LEADERSHIP * Leadership, management, and operating styles	Difference in expectation and response	
* Use of power, control, and authority	Perceived lack or abuse of	
* Changes without preparation of, discussion among, and ownership by the people	Perceived absence of	
* Reward and incentives	Inadequate or punishing	
* Monitoring processes	Inadequate	
OTHERS		

Appendix F

Survey of Forced Termination Questionnaire
Compiled by: Norris E. Smith
LifeWay Christian Resources
Pastor-Staff Leadership
Southern Baptist Convention

In a 1996, 1997, 1998, Directors of Missions were surveyed and asked: "In your experience, what are the most common causes of forced termination?"
The five leading causes are identical in each survey and in the same descending order.

First: Control issues - who's going to run the church
Second: Poor people skills on the part of the pastor
Third: Church's resistance to change
Fourth: Pastor's leadership style - too strong
Fifth: Church was already conflicted when the pastor arrived

Persons interested in resources for conflict resolution can contact the church-minister relations director of their State Baptist Convention or LeaderCare at LifeWay Christian Resources, 127 Ninth Ave., N., Nashville, TN 37234-0166. Main number, (615)251-2000.

Those interested in information concerning the Survey of Forced Termination Questionnaire can contact the Pastoral Staff Leadership department at the above address and at (615)251-2000, or www.lifeway.com.

Appendix G

Commission on Ministry Report
Survey of Forced Termination Questionnaire
Baptist State Convention of North Carolina
Cary, North Carolina
Winter, 1998

1. Pastors were asked: "What did you consider to be the primary reason for being forced to resign or terminated? (Only top four reasons were ranked):

First: Control issues - who is running the church
Second: Pre-existing conflict in the church
Third: Congregation's resistance to change
Fourth: Lack of trust and respect

2. Lay persons were asked: "What do you consider the primary reason(s) for resignation or forced termination? (Only top four reasons were ranked):

First: Minister determined to control everything
Second: Lack of interpersonal skills on the part of the minister —breakdown in communication, inappropriate confrontations, etc.
Third: Lack of pastoral ministry— visitation to homes, hospitals, etc.
Fourth: Lack of mutual trust and respect

Persons interested in the full "Commission on Ministry Report" should contact:

Baptist State Convention of North Carolina
Wayne Oakes, Consultant with Pastoral Ministries (Church Conflict)
Fred McGehee, Sr. Consultant in Pastoral Ministries
P.O. Box 1107 Ph. (800) 395-5102
Cary, NC 27512 www.bscnc.org

It is recommended that church leaders and congregations study and utilize this report as well as other surveys and reports conducted by denominations and other organizations that are concerned about the health and well-being of church leaders and congregations.

Appendix H

YOUR CHURCH Special Report
Forced Exits: "A Too-Common Ministry Hazard"

by John C. LaRue, Jr.
Your Church Magazine: March/April 1996, 72.

John C. LaRue, Jr. explains this report by saying, "We mailed 999 surveys to a random selection of U.S. pastors who subscribe to *Leadership, Christianity Today, and Your Church.* A total of 593 pastors responded, giving a 59 percent response rate. With a sample this size, results are considered accurate to within plus or minus 4 percentage points 95 percent of the time."

LaRue sees "forced exits" as a chronic problem among congregations. He says, "Nine out of ten pastors (91%) know three to four others who have been forced out of pastoral positions. In fact, one-third of all pastors (34%) serve congregations who either fired the previous minister or actively forced his or her resignation. Perhaps more telling, nearly one-fourth (23%) of all current pastors have been forced out at some point in their ministry. Many who are forced out do not return to a ministry position: Ten percent of dismissed predecessors left pastoral ministry."

Reasons for Forced Exit:

46% Pastors cite conflicting visions for the church as the greatest source of tension between them and lay leaders.
38% Personality conflicts (with congregations and/or church boards)
32% Unrealistic expectations (by both pastors and congregations)
24% Unclear expectations
22% Personality conflicts among church staff
21% Theological differences

19% Personality conflict with senior pastor

Finally, terminated pastors indicated they had had more misconceptions about ministry expectations than had other pastors (32% vs. 21%).

Your Church Magazine Ph. (630)260-6200
465 Gundersen Drive
Carol Stream, Illinois 60188

For information on all five articles concerning "Forced Exits" contact:
John LaRue,Jr. Ph. (630)260-6200
Christianity Today www.Christianitytoday.com
465 Gundersen Dr.
Carol Stream, ILL 60188

Appendix I

How to control your anger.

by

Tim LaHaye, *Anger Is a Choice*, (Grand Rapids: Zondervan, 1982), 156.

1. **GET MORE INFORMATION:** Information can change thoughts and feelings. Oftentimes what is perceived or assumed is not really happening at all.

2. **OPEN YOUR MEMORY FILE:** Hurt and anger from past experiences can continue to affect you now. Identify these. Don't let them trigger you.

3. **EVALUATE:** Are there common times, people, or associations that "trigger" your outbursts? If so, learn to avoid or be careful in these situations.

4. **FACE YOUR ANGER:** Trying to justify it, explain it, or blame someone else makes you incurable. You are responsible for your actions.

5. **EXPRESS IT SOONER:** Don't let negative feelings fester. Get over situations sooner. Express yourself before anger takes hold.

6. **THINK POSITIVELY:** The mind must dwell on something, so feed it positive emotional food.

7. **RECOGNIZE DISPLACED ANGER:** Most of the time people are angry about one thing but take their anger on others who are not connected to it. Discover the real root cause of your anger.
8. **CONFESS AND REPENT:** When you do "lose it," ask forgiveness of the people involved and of God.

LaHaye concludes, "Anger is a habit...that can control a person as tenaciously as heroin or cocaine making them react inwardly and outwardly in a selfish manner." He continues, "You need not remain a slave to this or any other habit. We have at our disposal the power of the Spirit of God to help us."

From: Bob Harrison, *Power Points for Success* (Tulsa: Honor Books, 1997), 69-70.

Appendix J

The Intentional Interim Ministry

A vital option for churches in transition

I was fortunate to be in the first group of ministers who were trained in the Southeast to minister to churches that are in transition or in the interim period following the loss of a pastor. The training was provided by The Center for Congregational Health,® which is a part of The School of Pastoral Care at the Wake Forest University Baptist Medical Center in Winston-Salem, North Carolina. The group of ministers from several denominations that underwent the specific training formed the Association of Intentional Interim Ministers (AIIM). Since entering the pastoral ministry in 1979, I have found my work as an Intentional Interim Minister (IIM) to be the most rewarding ministry I've ever experienced. I believe the intentional interim process can be the most effective and helpful ministry available to churches today. This type of ministry is especially helpful to churches in transition and churches that have experienced a painful history and are in need of healing. The IIM can also be a positive and encouraging experience for churches that want to become healthier, more vibrant, and more focused in their ministry and mission. Good marriages can become better, and so can congregations.

> According to the Center for Congregational Health: ® Significant studies of hundreds of interim congregations over the past twenty years are now showing that the interim period between pastors can be an important time in congregational life. R. Neil Chafin, an experienced consultant to congregations, says, "The way a con-gregation chooses to use its interim time will shape congregational growth, identity, and health for years to come. We also know that what is done

in the interim time really determines whether the new minister and congregation will form a sold ministry team.

Congregations that fail to make wise use of interim time tend to repeat their history with the new minister. This can lead to pain and confusion for the minister and prevent the congregation from meeting its goals of spiritual growth."

For more information concerning the Intentional Interim Ministry process, contact:

Robin Danner
Center for Congregational Health
Medical Center Boulevard
Winston-Salem, NC 27157-1098

Office: (336)716-9722
Fax: (336)716-9875
Congreg@wakehealth.edu
www.Healthchurch.org

Appendix, K

How Rev. Dennis J. Hester can help:

Dennis James Hester is an ordained Southern Baptist minister and serves as an Intentional Interim Minister, church consultant, workshop leader, conference speaker and personal coach to individuals, groups, congregations, non-profit organizations.

Rev. Hester is available to help individuals, churches, groups and non-profit organizations in

- Helping churches to benefit during transitions and preparation to call a new pastor
- Training Pastor Search Committees in finding and creating a climate for success
- Building and maintaining relationships at home, school, church and in the work placenby teaching The Role Reconciliation Model
- Equipping churches to grow and minister in the new millennium
- Helping to develop mission statements for individuals, churches and other groups
- Leadership training for pastor, staff and church leaders.

Conducting Seminars on the following topics:

- "Making Good Churches Better"
- "How to Keep From Getting Fired as a Pastor or Staff Person"
- "Learning Why Church Members and Employees 'Drop Out'"
- "Learning to Make Sense of Life's Transitions and Other Important Changes"
- "Staying Power: How Christians Can Be Better Employees, and Employers and How to Leave a Lasting Witness in the Secular Workplace"
- "How to Maintain Emotional and Spiritual Health"
- "How to Deal with "Difficult People," and How to Appreciate Their Differences"
- "How to Work Through Grief, Anger and Personal Crisis"
- "Learning How to Manage and Resolve Conflict"
- "Learning How to "Hold Out" and Avoid "Burning Out," and "Rusting Out""

For speaking, tailor-made workshops, consulting and personal coaching for individuals, congregations, non-profit groups or business please contact: Dennis@Dennishester.com.

About the Author

Dennis Hester has pastored churches in North and South Carolina and Virginia. He has served as a chaplain, revivalist and volunteer missionary. He is the author of numerous articles and newspaper columns and has compiled several books on the late famous NC evangelist, Vance Havner. In his community, he has volunteered with the Abuse Prevention Council; been a mentor for divinity students at Gardner-Webb University's School of Divinity; and taught "Communication in the Work Place" and "Customer Service" at his local community college for non-profit organizations and for small businesses.

A graduate of Gardner-Webb College (now University), Southeastern Baptist Theological Seminary and Oklahoma Baptist Medical Center's Clinical Pastoral Education Program, he is certified as an Intentional Interim Minister by the Center for Congregational Health of the School of Pastoral Care, Baptist Hospital in Winston-Salem, NC.

Dennis now devotes his time to writing, consulting, leading workshops and coaching individuals church groups and non-profit organizations in leadership and people skills.

Dennis is married to Pam King Hester, who is a Certified Nurse Midwife and former foreign missionary to Zimbabwe. Africa. She recently retired from a health care clinic she owned and operated in Forest City, NC, called "Mountain Laurel Women's Health Care. Dennis and Pam live in Winston-Salem, NC, and their son, Nathan, and their daughter, Rachael live in North Carolina also.

Dennis is presently Intentional Interim Pastor at Union Cross Baptist Church in Kernersville, NC.

RESOURCES AND CONTACT INFORMATION

WHAT OTHERS ARE SAYING ABOUT THIS BOOK

"Pastor, We Need to Talk!" asks the questions that any pastor or local congregation needs to answer in order to avoid the epidemic sweeping this nation of pastoral forced exits. Well-researched, practical steps are offered to help churches and ministers resolve conflict with compassion before it's too late.

John LaRue
Vice President ChristianityToday.com, Christianity Today International

Dennis Hester has touched a nerve spot in today's church scene: inner conflict that prevents the church from fulfilling its outward mission. I found the book to be realistic, insightful, helpful and informative. Applying some of his suggestions to our churches today will put us on the right track toward reconciliation and retooling for ministry.

Brian Harbour
Author and Pastor of First Baptist Church, Richardson, TX

This book help congregations and pastors communicate under stressful conditions. There are lots of ideas and checklists to use as a guide for managing conflict.

Speed B. Leas
Senior Consultant with Alban Institute

"Pastor, We Need to Talk!" is direct, with helpful illustrations from congregational life. It is laced with pertinent biblical references. We

believe many pastors, church lay leaders and members will find it useful.

.Rod L. Reinecke and Ruth R. Wright
Church consultants and trainers with ConTrOD Associates

I have worked with Dennis on a church staff and I know his love for the local church and for pastors. He has a passion for helping churches and church leaders know how to resolve conflicts that inevitably arise in any congregation. This passion is evident in his book, which is written as a very practical guide for both church leaders and staff. I highly recommend it.

Dr. Alice Cullinan
Professor of Religion and Religious Education, Gardner-Webb University;
Author of *Time for a Checkup: Assessing our Progress in Spiritual Growth,*
Christian Literature Crusade

"Pastor, We Need to Talk!" should grace the shelves of every church library. Anyone, from the layman to the local Pastor, including denominational leaders, would find Hester's 'cookbook approach' to dealing with the timeless, every-increasing problem of strained pastor-church relations both down-to-earth, straightforward and easy to follow.

Edward W. McCann
Deacon, Jonesboro Baptist Church, Roseland, VA

Each year, hundreds of congregations come to grief due to conflict with their pastoral leadership. From out of this tragic church experience, Dennis

Hester has written a very helpful book. Here is a book that gives us practical guidance in dealing with church conflict, particularly conflict in leadership. Congregations and pastors would do well to read Hester before they talk to one another about their differences. Then they can talk to one another like Christians—which is what it's all about anyway. This is a great resource for pastors and churches in conflict and before conflict occurs.

William H. Willimon
Dean of the Chapel and Professor of Christian Ministry
Duke University, Durham, NC

I am glad that Dennis has written this resource, which is readable, warm, challenging and insightful. If church leaders will use *"Pastor, We Need to Talk!"* it will help bring conflict to a redemptive closure.

Norris Smith
Pastor-Staff Leadership Department
Lifeway Christian Resources for the SBC

Do not put this book on a bookshelf, but keep it on your desk to review over and over again. You will soon discover that ideas from it will keep cropping up in your thoughts, behaviors and the way you treat others. Make it a gift to yourself. Remember that every person is radically gifts and radically flawed. Be sure to say thanks for the gifts and to forgive the flaws.

John Savage
John Savage Resources LLC

His Way Publishing appreciates your interest in its products and welcomes your comments concerning this book.

If you would like to have a future book to address a special need, please write and tell us:
HisWayPublishingcustomerservice.ebooks@gmail.com.

www.ingramcontent.com/pod-product-compliance
Lightning Source LLC
LaVergne TN
LVHW021500080426
835509LV00018B/2354